WARBLING IN THE WIND

SURYANSH S. CHAUHAN

ISBN 979-888591226-6

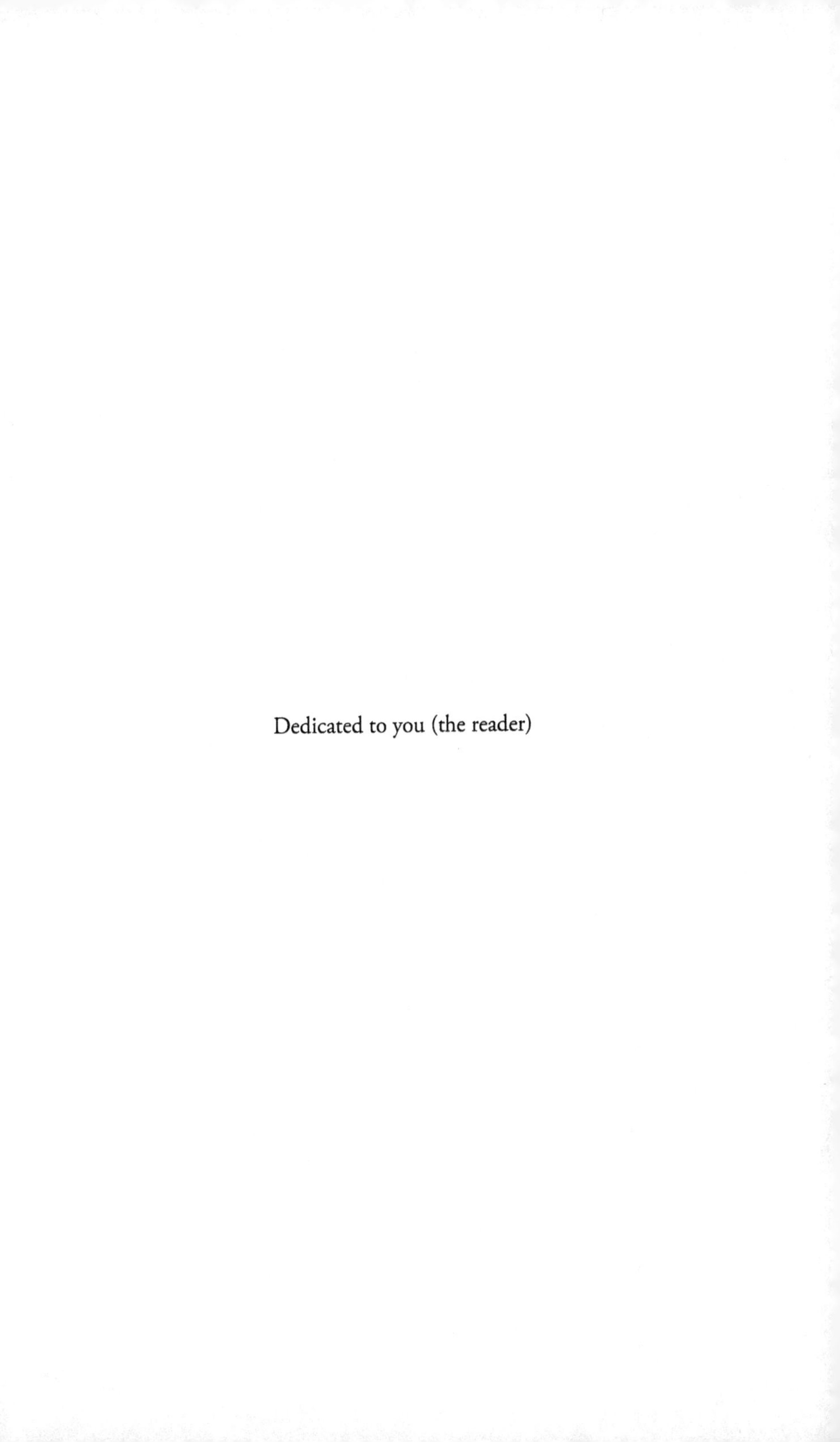

Dedicated to you (the reader)

Contents

Contents

Contents

Preface

After the "florio-trilogy" and 2 anthologies, I'm, back with another solo poetry compilation. I hope the content lives well up to your expectations as I've put my heart into it.

Acknowledgements

The previous books gave me a whole lotta encouragement to write more & more poems for my dearest readers and mostly for myself.

My parents and friends have been like pillars throughout the whole journey and I'm glad to have them by my side. I hope the blessings remain by my said and the pen never runs out of ink to write.

Prologue

Warbling in the wind, soothing my soul...

I wake-up to the sweet melody everyday,

And watch these birds return to their home in the evening

About The Author

Suryansh Chauhan (going by the pen name : Suryansh S. Chauhan) hails from the city of Gwalior, Madhya Pradesh (Born : 29th May, 2004).

This teenager is a student at DAV Kota. Apart from writing, he also has a great deal of interest in painting and photography. He's also a national level karate player & YouTuber for fun.

He started writing at the age of 14 and got published as a co-author at the age of 15 and then as a solo author at the age of 16. He believes that writing is all about framing one's own feelings, emotions or imagination in a way that it brings a sense of peace.

A lot of his poems are pretty long, simple and explanatory as if they're almost a song. He writes to express; for relief. Because he believes that art in any form is a therapy in itself.

Social Media—

Instagram : @suryansh_s_chauhan & @thefadingbud_

Twitter : @Surya_S_Chauhan

Youtube : Suryansh S Chauhan

Mail : surya29.sc@gmail.com

The following poems(1-29) are the ones I wrote initially but chose not to include in the previous books for various reasons most common of them was...um let's say... they seemed to be nice back then but it feels a bit weird reading "the old me" now.

1. Still I Stand Strong

You think you've lagged me behind ,
But I'm sorry to say that you're wrong.
You've tried to weaken me;
Shatter me & scatter me,
But still here I am, standing strong.
There's only one way to settle this;
once & for all.
Let's do it my way,
No matter night or day.
I'll walk alone & conquer the quest,
In the journey to be the very best.
You may try but you ain't gonna win,
At last, you'll have to pay for your every single sin.

2. Anger

Undermining it leads to the arrival of trouble,
It increases problems infact turns them double.
It has the potential to break relations,
Start a massive war between nations.
The emotion that surpasses others,
Can be a result of unfulfilled temptations.
Anger is injurious, anger is deadly.
and that's the truth, according to my observations.
it isn't the deadliest weapon for sure,
But still anger has got no cure.
For some it's a way to express their love,
For some it's a way to remove their frustration
Love needs time but anger requires only a mere moment,
Anger is the endgame not just a demonstration.

3. Flame

A little spark grew vast,
spreading devastation, destroying lives.
He kept gazing at the fierce fire,
if he'd survive then he'll remember this
as a really painful past.
Symbol of destruction & Anger,
Yes it is the fire.
which also represents lust & desire.
Millions of memories turned into ashes,
Everything was engulfed with flame.
His home, his family, everything was gone,
Deep down his heart did moan.
Everything was burnt & shattered,
Nothing was left except the stone(s).

4. Dear Problems,

Dear problems,
I don't know what the hell is wrong with you,
I guess we're kinda together forever.
I don't want you,but I guess that you do,
C'mon I'm way too dumb to handle you,
go find someone clever.
I've been in a million problems till the date,
So let me be happy for a single moment,
Please wait!
What if i say that this isn't working anymore,
Leave me then, will you?
Oh, of course not!
Will you ever let happiness knock my life's door?
Let's do a quick countdown,
From one-to-three
Oh god! I'm exhausted
Atleast now set me free.

5. Back To Me?

I know it's hard to,
But i wish you could come back to me.
I wish i could see you once again,
the shimmer in your eyes once more.
I wish we could meet once again,
on the lonely sea shore.
Not much to talk about,
— well except for our silly jokes.
Nothing remained the same as before,
different dreams, different goals.
We had no option but to part ways,
No more "us" No more "we"
Now it's just,
separate you & separate me.

6. No-One

No one to lay beside,
'cause no one stood
You too left me,
when you could.
No shoulder to cry on,
No reason to carry on.
Unable to move on,
When you left me alone.
No one to hold my hand,
no one to console.
all i have with me is a bucket full of
false promises and broken trust.

7. If There Was A Way

If there was a way,
you could still be mine.
If there was a way,
we could chat again at 9.
If there was a way,
we could make it work
If there was a way,
I could stop being a jerk
If there was a way,
Where you could stay.
If there was a way,
I wouldn't have let it go away.

8. Childhood

Childhood
When...
School bags were heavy,
our hearts were not.
Notebooks were numerous,
problems were not.
Playing all the time with friend(s),
our mischiefs never end.
Those were the days of happiness; of joy,
humans were valued; not considered as toy(s).
Chocolates were our favorite,
competition was not.
We were taught to love,
we were taught to pray.
Instead we learned to hate,
we learned to slay.
We were like little plants back then,
Which have now turned into a tree.
Time changed; Priorities changed,
So did we.

9. Doesn't Affect Me Anymore

I've learnt from my pain,

Because earlier, I preferred heart over Brain.

Experienced losses and gains,

Suffering is in my veins.

So i tied my heart with chains,

To prevent emotional drain(s).

Exhausted as hell,

Still was standing there.

Nothing felt well,

After all I've bear-ed.

Life became slow,

My mood remained dull & low.

Kinda sad, kinda depressed,

Kinda tangled, kinda perplexed.

But now, this comes out from my heart's core,

That's it doesn't affect me anymore.

10. Being Alone Isn't So Lonely After all

Being alone isn't so lonely after all,
when there's no one yours to call.
All you have is silence & questions,
Where to go now? Which direction?
Life is a blank sheet and the colours are in your hands
Which one to fill? You may ask.
It's quite tough to decide,
Indeed a tangling task.
Life is too long to measure,
and too short to live.
Sometimes we hurt others,
a few forget and a few forgive.
Noting is permanent,
So be happy with your contemporary life.
When people walk away from you,
there's no need to be sad.
Because it isn't your fault,
It's their choice.
Change begins with today,
It doesn't require an occasion.
Because it is an opportunity,
And there's no need to be sad because
Being alone isn't so lonely after all
(When you have your 'Self' with you)

11. Just One Step

C'mon it ain't that hard after all,
Just one step; move along with me.
You'll get hurt, you'll feel sad,
But it'll be for your good only.
You'll face many problems,
Difficulties would be plenty.
Don't lose hope, It'll be hard
but still a beautiful journey.
There's so much to learn,
so much to explore.
Let positivity flow through your mind,
Open the closed doors.
There'll be tough times, quite frightening
You've gotta build your courage above the lightning??
Giving up too early is the biggest regret,
Your time is now, on your mark, get, set
Go! One step, just one step is all
what it takes to fulfill your destiny.

12. Slow & Steadily

Step by step; I've learnt to walk slow & steadily,
I've been running from myself for years and now I'm exhausted.
Still I'm standing strong yet breathing heavily.
Losing ain't an option for me,
'cause I've came a long way to attain victory.
I'm here to make history,
Trying to solve life which itself is a mystery.
No need to introduce myself,
soon you'll know my name.
I don't follow the rules,
'cause I am the whole game.
Success is my milestone,
I'm a Lion, not a dog that you can tame.
I'm born to rule, not to stand in the lines,
I'm a rare diamond, extracted from mines.
I'm different, I'm one of a kind.
I'm hard to be understood by your small mind.
You're no one to tell me what to do
I am my own boss, not you!
©?:@suryansh_s_chauhan

13. Broken

A broken heart that was still beating,

Through such a long time, she had been cheating.

Maybe my efforts, maybe my love wasn't enough.

This betrayal felt like a huge load on my heart,

As if I was the target and she had a dart.

It's quite a long story,

From where should I even start?

My heart felt empty as if there was a crater,

The one whom I truly loved, turned out to be traitor.

All the beautiful memories & quality time spent together instantly vanished,

My dreams, my love, my trust, all were finished.

My closest friend, my dearest companion was now nothing more than my enemy.

I suffered from so much pain, and she didn't even bother to look at me.

It seems like she was an expert in this regime

14. The Fault In Our Stars

Probably there's a fault in our stars,
That's why we're so close and yet so far.
Every second passes in regret,
I wish we would've never met.
Still i pray for you to be alright,
hope for your future to be bright.
Still I wanna know whether you're okay or not,
Nostalgia hits me when I pass by out meeting spot.
I would have tried harder, if you'd ask me to,
Although the end wasn't well.
But it's neither because of you,
Nor because of me.
Probably there's a fault in our stars;
Which stops you & me to be together as 'we',
Maybe it's nothing but our destiny.
I'd have tried harder, if you'd ask me to,
although the end wasn't well,
maybe a state worse than hell,
It's neither because of you,
nor because of me,
It's only because of the fault in our Stars; our destiny.

15. School Desk

Oh! there it is : the school desk
on which we used to sit.
on which we've created
numerous memories.
on which we drew lines,
and wrote names.
on which studied together,
and played games.
Either Penfighting, bookcricket or
hitting someone with rubber band,
we were together in everything,
our childishness is something only we remember,
Alnd only we can understand.

16. Blackboard

A blank blackboard is an
opportunity; an invitation,
An open door for innovation.
A blackboard creates the
future of students :
The younger generation.
It is there for learning,
It is there for education.
It demands your focus,
your attention.
It demands your interest,
your concentration.
Though a few children ignore it
because they're lost in their own imagination.

17. Chalk

A teacher's wand, a blackboard's mate.

Which helps the user to write

Even though it causes it's own fate.

But what if I tell you that people are like chalk...

you won't believe me, but hear me out.

watch my words, because for me they're my voice, my shout.

They used me, they used me as if I was a chalk.

And after all their intentions were fulfilled, they decided to walk away.

Pretended to be someone who's never done something wrong.

Behaved like a criminal who's killed someone and acts if everything's fine.

18. Rape

Not every Cinderella loses her heels,

Patriarchy doesn't hail anymore and no woman kneels.

Damini, Asifa, Nirbhaya, Priyanka, Manisha.

Aren't they enough?

To prove that monsters have taken birth on this earth.

This country is our motherland,

But for women safety, no one wants to take a stand.

Rapists aren't men... they're those who don't know how to behave,

Love is extinct, Lust is all what they crave.

For a pleasure of few minutes they force a woman,

And when it isn't enough they even take her life.

Without thinking she too is a woman,

Someone's mother, sister, daughter or wife.

Prostitute, Whore, slut. by such names she is called...

Why aren't men ever blamed?

These characterless men aren't even eligible to be called men or even human.

Still there's no penalty for this inhumane action and all we get from our government is a blank reaction.

Women rights are ignored,

Women safety? What does that even mean?

Who should be blamed for this?

The victim? The rapist? Or the government?

No one knows...why to burn candles

Why not burn the rapists...

19. Miles To Walk Before I Sleep

Ain't this one another long journey,
Haven't you suffered like this before
Miles to walk before I sleep,
I'll have to stand strong therefore.
Lookin' outta the window,
Tons of fascinating scenarios.
And I've found an escape,
While my eyes are working like a videotape.
When people are into their phones,
I'm embracing the nature.
Elevating mountains & emanating rivers on the way,
While travelling through contrary zones.
Maybe I've fallen in love with myself,
Or maybe I'm going insane with the flow.
Miles to walk before I sleep,
So here I go!

20. Tragic-Trait

Betrayal is like one of your trait,
since when has this been going inside your head?
Suffering for months,
finally i decided to let it go.
'cause enough of hurting myself,
for someone's who doesn't even care.
Billions of people on this planet,
but you were the one that i met.
was this some kind of a lesson,
or only a tragic that i regret.
Thousands of options,
yet i fell for you.
And look at us now,
we don't even talk like we used to do.
How do you even get the guts to call me by my name,
when my love, for you, was a mere game.
Just answer me, was it even worth it?
Like a cliché story in a modern world doesn't fit.

21. Champion

]It's only the beginning,

and you're miles away from winning.

The way is long, it'll buffer

pain on the way.

Be ready to suffer,

each & everyday.

Tie your shoelace,

get ready for the race.

Be prepared for loss too,

just in case.

It takes years of hard work,

a champion isn't prepared in a matter of days.

Go beyond the limits,

and hit the wickets.

The stadium is full,

sold out all tickets.

People are cheering your name,

Stand strong like a lone wolf & focus on your game.

All your sweat, all your blood

will pay back as your success & fame.

22. Finished. Fucked Up. Failure.

Now I've realized that my whole life was a lie.

And everyone I've met are different people in disguise.

Fire or ice, whatever ends the world

shall do it really quick. S you!-Robert Frost

And I'm done with the shit,

that the world throws at me everyday.

I am tired and i want to die,

where peace reside.

I don't wanna join this crowd of 7billion,

where I'm just a name that nobody knows.

What is this family? and why do i have it?

Even when i haven't asked for this.

What is the purpose of my life that serves,

and what is the worth that I deserve.

In a world running on money,

values are trash that doesn't matter.

Why am i even alive?

Why am i like this?

Why am i a failure?

Why am i fucked up?

and i am finished.

23. Would I Be What I Am Today?

Would I Be What I Am Today?

If I decided to remain unknown,

If I didn't have the courage to ask you out.

If you didn't decide to play with my feelings,

If you decided not to break my heart.

If I decided to stay away,

Would I be what I am today.

I'm incomplete without you,

and I'm broken because of you.

You were the one who shattered me,

and it took me years to find the pieces.

Yet I'm more precious than ever,

without you would this be possible? oh never!

Thy are the reason of me being the real me that i lost,

Maybe to learn to love myself, you were the cost.

I thought you were the one that I need,

but the rose i loved, turned out to be weed.

Toxic—yet i didn't leave,

for all of my love, It's only pain that I've received.

The thorns stabbed me and i did bleed tears out of my veins,

I wondered why am i so low?

Maybe it was because a rope was tied to my neck,

And I refused to let it go.

24. The Marbles of Achievement

Whatever I've achieved,

is the sole result of the lessons.

The lessons I've learnt,

from the pain that i received.

These achievements weren't easily obtained,

as if Marbles given to a rich toddler.

I've obtained them like a poor yet honest one,

walking on the streets with my bare feet & empty stomach.

No supporter was there until i announced my first victory,

and after that they claim to have known the entire history.

I begged for their support, while half of them ignored

There were still a few who stood by my side.

The ones who kept favouring me for good,

trying their best to help me grow.

They deserve the credit for my fame,

they are the efforts & support system behind my name.

A heartily Thankyou!♥? Keep Supporting!

~ @suryansh_s_chauhan

25. Story That'll Never End

Despite being miles apart,

you still reside inside my heart.

And if you ever feel low,

Just tightly hold the pillow

Imagining I am there with you.

And if you feel sad, don't hold your tears.

Cry it out, you'll feel light.

Remember one thing

that you might've heard before,

from a lot of people, but I mean it.

And it might sound cliché,

But still I gotta say

I love you♥?

I want to travel the world with you,

I wanna put my head on your shoulder,

and then you'd tilt to rest yours on mine.

We will lose in the loop of time.

If we were to meet differently in the past,

I don't know If I would still love you.

But I know if anything happens from now on,

I'd stand by your side no matter what.

I'm the writer and you're my poem

and this is our story that'll never end.

And I want this to go on & on, always & forever♥?

26. Stronger Than Ever

My breath is gradually slipping away,
And the world goes on it's own pace.
I don't know whether to rest
or to join back the race.
It's so tough to get back to normal again,
but I have to stand up.
There's greatness that awaits me,
Adventures that I need to go on.
Dates that I need to remember,
People I have to take care of.
Changes that I have to undergo,
And places I have to pass by.
The spark is still alive,
I just have to increase it.
So that when the fire shows up,
I'll be stronger than ever.

27. Power

Desire to dominate,
driving you crazy,
Corrupting innocence.
Limitless hunger &
Lust for power,
It's never enough.
You can attain power
But at what cost?
Courage or Sacrifice?
What makes you a hero?
Is faith only for the weak,
Or is It something that holds you together when everything's against
you.
What is power?
In it's absolute form.
Is it all to have?
Or nothing to care about?
If it's all there is,
Then who owns it?
Flawed, inappropriate, mediocre,
Who crave for it?
With what intent do you seek power?
Approval, Domination or Vengeance?
In the hands of evil,
Invites destruction,

To maintain balance,
The 'good' must be powerful too.
But the cycle goes on without partiality,
For as long as the world exists.
There's good in evil, and evil in good,
And good shall prevail...?

28. Dreams Of Utopia

Parents patting on the back,
And saying "I'm proud of you"
Hugging me and telling me,
that I'm important.
Receiving letters of love,
And being essential to someone.
Being useful to the world,
and loving myself.
Travelling the world,
taking things off the bucket list.
Not being afraid,
Living on my own,
A life with tranquility.
Being acknowledged,
appreciated and accepted.
What else could I ask for?
Being at peace with myself.
And smiling wholeheartedly,
Is all that I wished for.
I want the excitement back,
Which I once felt before.
All I have for now is numbness,
And dreams of utopia.

29. Back To Strangers

Tryna talk,
But what's there left.
Back to strangers,
I won't open up ever again,
You don't even care.
Tangled,
caught up in confusion,
Sorry to bother you with my existence.
As you spent time with me,
You must have realised...
And you continue to regret it,
Don't you?
Aight enough oversharing!
Maybe one day,
we'll meet again.
Like that weird dream,
Maybe now I know what It actually meant.
I decided that If I'm going to end up hurting myself,
I better enjoy it now,
Atleast it'll be worth it.
And now the pleasure's gone,
all there's left is pain.
My requirement for constant reassurance,
this demand leads to much more trouble.
Argh! It doesn't matter anymore,

I need a break from being myself.

30. Mystery

A dream of yours,
Where all the faces are blurred.
A distant future,
With lights too bright.
I can't see much,
But it feels familiar.
A place where I've been before,
With the people I haven't met yet.
As I run to catch the light,
At the end of the tunnel...
It vanishes,
Leaving me in the middle of nowhere.
Maybe it goes back to the sky,
Hovering on the horizon.
As a smile flashed in front me,
My eyes went blank.
Forcing me out of this world
...into reality.
Entry mentioned in my journal,
Life goes on as normal.
But the dream remains...
A mystery to me.

31. Letters

An envelope lying around,
With a pile of letters.
With stories full of love,
From teenagers to old couples.
Be it a proposal for date,
Or a plan to elope.
The mailman is evident,
Of a lot of faces smiling...
Or bursting into tears of joy,
Upon receiving a letter from their loved ones.
Such is the world,
Vast yet full of similiar stories.
But each one has it's uniqueness,
Some are like roses fading together.
Some are like sunflowers,
Facing the sun.
Some are like lotuses,
Surrounded in mud.
But each love story blooms,
And that's what makes them special.

32. Wine

Oh your sweet love
Is like an untouched bottle of fine wine.
Waiting for decades,
Waiting to be opened.
Unnoticed,
Untouched.
Years and years,
Passing by in the blink of an eye.
If I were to summarise our story,
It'd be a mere montage with seconds of you.
And the rest of the film,
Without your glimpse.
A love story without love,
Isn't it tragic.
Like a candy without sugar,
And a wizard without magic.
Like a cuisine without spice,
And ice tea without ice.
Like surviving cold winters without the sun,
Like living a life without any fun.
Such is your love,
Isn't it tragic.
A bottle of wine,
Untouched...

Waiting to be opened,
To reveal the magic.

33. Interwined

A fragrance that
You remember.
Amidst all those
Foggy memories.
And the warmth
You long for in the winters.
Like the sun
To the sunflowers
Oh I wanna be reason
You start believing in love.
I wanna be the home
You'll always wanna come back to.
An exciting weekend plan,
That you'll look forward to.
And a healthy routine,
You won't ever get tired of.
Spontaneous like
A last minute planned trip.
Through the highs and the lows,
Growing together like intertwined trees...

34. Honest

If we were to be
Honest for a sec,
I really wanna be
More than "just friends"
If you promise me that
You won't hate me,
I wanna confess...
But losing you...
Isn't worth the risk.
If we were to be
honest for a sec,
I really wanna take you away
Where we can be "together"
If you promise me that
You won't hate me,
I wanna let you know
Everything I love about you...
But again...
Losing you...
Isn't worth the risk.
The upcoming days
will break us apart,
I wish I could go back
And meet you sooner than I had.

Prolonged conversations,
Where we lose topics
And there's nothing left to talk about
Still, I don't want 'em to end at all...
So... let's be honest for a sec
Here comes the thing
I've always wanted to say
I really really like you...
And i wanna be more than
"just friends"
...is it really worth the risk?

35. Transit Love

Intoxicated nights,
spilling secrets
Opening up our hearts
and getting closer than ever
Blushing while reading texts
Falling asleep after each other's
Goodnight messages
But does it even matter....
If we'll end up
Forgetting each other...
Like a bad trip
That you never wanted to go on
Transit love,
Hurts more
Than it heals
And at this point,
I don't wanna be abandoned...
And i don't wanna be
Vulnerable again
Bottling up my emotions,
I've come this far...
If I let it all out
I'd be someone else.
And maybe,
You won't like that...

But does it even matter....
If we won't remember each other.

36. With You

The crescent that
Glows on your forehead
And open hair which
Blow in rhythm with the wind
Dancing in the moonlight
Just the two of us
And i don't want anyone
To come in between
Like an inside joke,
we can use at all gatherings
And they'd think to themselves,
What are they, a married couple?
And then we'd blush
And look sideways
Hiding our happiness
And embarrassment...
Oh my dreams are quite
movie-ish you see...
And I'd love to be
The main character beside you.
I want something like this
A beautiful beginning
A bitter-sweet half
And the perfect ending...
With you.

37. Pearls

You got me smilin'
through the screen
Is this one outta your
arsenal of specialities
Chilly night passes by,
craving for your warmth
Can I do something
To turn everything around
I wish I had met you a bit earlier,
In that case i wouldn't have...
Made a lotta mistakes,
On my way to you.
A clear path in fog,
Bright light in haze.
Sun to the sunflower,
With radiant face.
The vibes you give off
And the things you say
How could someone
not fall in love with you?
Like pearls...
Gettin' out of the ocean.
Shining in the moonlight
Like stars.

And you smell just like
Lavender fields...
And you got me feeling
Like you're the one I need.

38. Just A Little Longer

I wish we could write more poems together,
Go on dates more often.
Talk a bit more,
And stay together just a little longer.
But things don't go how i want...
I guess that was it,
This short while has been
The most beautiful time of my life.
And I've felt grateful to be alive
At the point of time...
Which is kind of surprise
For someone like me
Always ranting about life.
However, if there's even the
Slightest possibility
Of meeting you again.
You know and so do I
That I'll never let it go...
It's not about the past or present
What bothers you is what bothers me
And it's the future;
The tomorrow that's ahead of us
And there's so much I wish I could do...
But i guess this is it for now
Time to bid farewell

You've been nothing but great, partner.

39. Can I Count You In?

Can we meet again
But this time...
A little earlier...
So we could have
Plenty of time at hand
Do the same things again
But i won't be shy anymore
Like last time.
Go to all those places,
You've been asking me to go to
Take pictures to fill our album.
Make playlists that never end
While we go on numerous roadtrips.
And I'll keep reassuring you
That you're the one.
Not just through words
But through actions too.
Handle your mood swings
And care for you.
Recite poems,
Share moments together.
You on the backseat
And we wander in the streets
Without knowing the direction

Captivated by your eyes

Lost there with no intention of returning.

Then you'll grab me tightly

And whisper something in my ear

There's a million things

I want to tell you

The list goes on & on...

Can I count you in?

40. Floating Log

A sensation of burnin'
on the inside
Kinda weird
As i was smiling
Just a second ago
All the things
That i liked once
Aren't the same anymore
It's annoying
To be in my own skin
So disgusting,
I want to crawl out
And k/ll myself
Trust the process?
I will never trust again.
Experiencing this
All over again?
I'd rather be a drowning ship
than a floating log
Belonging nowhere.

41. Mood Board

It all just feels like a crazy dream,
I never wanna wakeup from...
A beautiful movie sequence
With charismatic scenery...
And a song that
Everyone will sing along...
I like to be with you, partner.
Livin' in the moment and making memories...
Months apart,
you won't even be here...
So all I'm asking you
Is to be with me.
Make a hell lotta memories,
Live while we're young and live free.
Don't go around
Hurtin' me with those reality checks.
I know we only have
Limited time at our hand.
So instead of checklists,
Let's enjoy painting our moodboard <3

42. Good Enough?

Shitty poems,
Similiar themes.
Repeated words,
Shitty schemes.
You're never gonna be
good enough
Nothing but a self
proclaimed artist
Even a kid can write
better than you.
Boring topics,
Random Gibberish.
Zero efforts,
No creativity.
24/7 ranting,
Zero productivity.
A pen in hand,
And a paper to write.
Inspiring to others,
But good for nothing.
—Sweetie, you have no clue
What it feels to be like me.
To write a lot,
And hate everything.

To feel like a god,
Waiting for death.
To smile a lot,
And feel nothing.
Knowing that,
I'll never be good enough.

43. Hope

I'm not fundamentally a bad person
But I get overwhelmed sometimes.
Committing sins from time to time,
Things I can never tell anyone.
Filled with flaws, issues and insecurities,
An emotionless scumbag.
I wish that I could stop my past self
....from even existing.
Things just happen,
And we spend the rest of our lives...
Looking for a meaning,
Only to find out that there is none.
So here we are soaking in the rain,
Surrounded by dark clouds.
Waiting for the sun to shine again,
But who knows how long it'll take.
I'd rather die of cold,
Than to keep hope.
Something which I've lost
Long ago...

44. Today

Woke up and chose to be kind,
Fed a stray dog...
And didn't put too much burden
On my mind...
Oh little acts of self-love,
And treating myself right...
Even though life's short
Let's make it worthwhile
Days that aren't here yet,
Even if they're planned
They won't go accordingly
So let's not worry about tomorrow.
Live in the moment,
Drop all the worries & sorrow.
Breath deeply and live freely.
To love is to live
And to live is to love
And the world goes crazy....
The lights are blinking
Like a concert
In the middle of a desert.
It feels so senseless,
But it feels so good.
To not worry about tomorrow,
And to live today to its fullest.

45. Sweet Old Memory

A wooden house,
Somewhere in the hills.
Lying in the bed,
Enjoying your warmth...
But the scent too
Is slowly fading away
Just like your presence...
And i know
It was meant to be this way
Transit young love,
Full of feelings...
But without any future...
Mind full of imaginary scenarios.
Living in a dream,
That'll definitely end one day.
But I'll never forget you,
And the things you said...
I'll keep you with me,
Like a sweet old memory.
Maybe I'll see you someday again,
It'll be a nice little reunion.
Though I'll be a whole different me,
So be prepared because I won't...
Repeat the same mistakes,
Or cause harm to myself.

I'll be the strongest,
And the best version of me.

46. Almost Emotionless

Bit my lip on accident,
Even after all that happened
Still didn't feel anything
It's like i can't feel anything at all
I don't cry at funerals,
Feel sad on heartbreaks,
Get triggered by insults
Or be happy on my birthday.
Is it even living
If I'm not enjoying it
I don't think about anyone else
That's just how selfish I am.
Random strangers,
Close friends
Complicated relationships
And blood related ones
All of them are
the same to me
As if nothing
Or no-one matters to me
As if everyday is same
And i don't want anyone
To relate to this...
Please.

Long distance lovers,
Or friends...
Relationships that failed
And the ones that just vanished away...
I have to remember all of this,
Carry it on my back...
Weighing me down
But i know i can't complain
Even if i want to cry and confide,
I don't want anyone to know
So i write it out
And just keep ranting
Knowing that I'm so messed up,
Yet i still carry myself well.
Flooding emotions and
Not accepting them at all
I lie to myself everyday,
Saying that it's alright...
Even though I try to hide it
I don't wanna say...
As each day passes by
I'm becoming emotionless.

47. Happy Ending

Even I want love that stays,
Even I want to make efforts
That don't go to waste.
Even I want love that's not fake.
But is too much to ask for...
Even though i know that
You feel the same way for me,
It's really difficult to believe sometimes...
Meeting the right person
At the wrong time.
Another love story
Without a happy ending.
Call it off right now,
Or enjoy as long as it goes...
Enjoy it like a vacation,
Don't let it pass like a business trip.
Savour each moment,
Make a hell lotta memories...
So that we can think to ourselves,
All of it was worth it.
And meet again
One day....
Not like two awkward adults,
But like two childhood friends.

48. Middle

Smilin' with tears in my eyes,
I'm just glad that i got to meet you...
And 10 years from now,
You'll be living your dream life.
I hope something works out
Just fine for me as well...
Our worlds will be different,
And we won't meet again...
Before all that happens,
I just wanna let you know...
That the days we spent together,
And the dates we went on...
The secrets that we shared,
And everything we felt...
All of it was real to me,
And I'll have nothing but
Best wishes for you....
And thankyou for the memories.
You were neither my beginning,
Nor my end...
But you've been really great,
A "middle" that i won't forget.

49. Young Love

I keep thinking about you,
And i won't deny that...
I often dream of you,
And you keep crossing my mind..
Young love is all about
Feelings...
And we don't care about
Anything else.
The days with you
Are so much fun.
And I love being with you,
Isn't that enough?
There are things,
We say to eachother.
But can't say aloud
Or repeat...
Because it becomes
way too embarassing
For you and me....
Aren't we both
Glad to be together?
'cause that's what
Young love is all about.
Little things
That make us happy...

Witho worrying
About tomorrow.

50. Emotionless

Curious to uninterested,
How far have i come....
The last time when it happened,
It was like a trigger...
To work on myself,
And become better...
Pleasant times,
So much I've earned.
Harsh times,
So much I've learned.
But as time passed by,
There have been a lot of...
Unfortunate events.
Sometimes I'm high on happiness,
Sometimes I'm just numb...
And this time,
Even though i know...
How it'll end,
There's nothing i can do...
To stop it from happening.
A moment of happiness,
That'll vanish in an instant.
Going with the worst case scenario,
I'll end up way more cold than ever...

Removing the "almost" from
Almost emotionless.

51. Trash Poetry

High Hopes,
Forgotten dreams.
Weird expectations,
Silent screams.
Carrying heavy baggage,
Even with backpain.
Complicated emotions,
I just can't stay sane.
Rubbish poetry,
Awful paintings.
Desperate to scratch the walls,
Tear everything apart.
Like a maniac
On a rampage.
Things i don't like to talk about,
Flow in my poetry...
Like confessing my love,
To an old friend of mine...
Opening up after years
Of bottling up...
It sure feels weird,
And what else is weird...?
Ah yes, expectations...
And you ask why these poems
are trash...

Random drafts that i dump in books,
Full of mixed emotions...
That make no sense at all.

A Note By The Author

Keeping in mind the difference in each poem. It's wise to say that human emotions are quite complex to understand but once we establish a medium to know how we feel and what affects us, it can be miraculous.

The pleasure I get while writing drives me to write more and more. Essentially, it's for self-satisfaction but I'm honoured when people read my work and appreciate it.

One must not undermine the value of words for they are the very essence of our existence. What shapes us is our language, culture and heritage just like a mother.

Thankyou dear reader,
I hope to see you again next time.
Until then...farewell!...
~Suryansh S. Chauhan

Previous Works Of Suryansh S. Chauhan

The following books are a part of "Florio-Trilogy" by Suryansh S. Chauhan. Each book consists of 51 poems by the author:

• Published as an Author (solo) of the book 'The Fading Bud' (ISBN : 9781639202218) 10th May, 2021

• Published as an Author (solo) of the book 'The Evanescent Floret' (ISBN : 9781685236533) 11th August, 2021

• Published as an Author (solo) of the book 'The Dwindling Bloom' (ISBN : 9781685869939) 18th October, 2021

The following books are anthologies compiled by Suryansh S. Chauhan. Each book consists of 51 poems by various co-authors :

• Published as a compiler of the book 'Flame Petals' (ISBN : 9798885469609) 30th December, 2021

• Published as a compiler of the book 'Kavya Pankhudi' (ISBN : 9798885698719) 27th January, 2022

THE
FADING
BUD

Suryansh S. Chauhan

The Evanescent Floret

Suryansh S. Chauhan

The
Dwindling
Bloom
Suryansh S. Chauhan

Flame
Petals
Compiled by
Suryansh S. Chauhan

काव्य पंखुड़ी
कविता संग्रह
सूर्यांश एस. चौहान
(द्वारा कंपाईल्ड)

Thankyou For Reading!♥?

For

The well-wishers of my community

Who have inspired me all through

Every religious ideal has a historical time and context. The circumstances for its realization will not be sufficient to sustain any perpetual decree or pronouncement sustainably. The reform process is inevitable and is instrumental in bringing about a religious ideal and giving it dynamic momentum, inclusiveness, flexibility, etc. While the reform advocates change, we must remember that the underlying cultural nuances, particularly the last mile ones, ensure the dynamism that regulates the various balancing checks, preserving and safeguarding the existing values, norms, ideals, decrees, etc. and providing improvised means of implementing them simultaneously. It propagates gradual change in certain aspects of social, religious, ideological, etc. realms rather than in rapid, fundamental, or revolutionary ways. While the conservative opposition negates the possibility of reform, the radical reform rejects the feasibility of it. In the case of Islam, reform was not a decisive event like the Protestant Reformation of European Christianity but rather a revolution that evolved through cycles of events throughout several centuries. Islam remains a staggeringly diverse and complicated religion in its geographical and political reach, making reforms difficult.

CONTENTS

1. ISLAM IS SIMPLE; MUSLIMS HAVE MADE IT HARD

An authentic saying of the Prophet Muhammad emphasises: "Religion is straightforward, and whoever overburdens himself in his religion will not be able to continue in that way. So you should not be extremists, but try to be near perfection and receive the good tidings and will be rewarded." (Bukhari Fath-ul-Bari, Page 102, Vol 1)

In the above hadith or prophetic saying, religion refers to the broader notion of Islam, that is, deen, a complete code encompassing every facet of human life. Deen comprises imaan (faith), Islam (practice) and Ihsan (a sense of social responsibility borne out of religious convictions).

The concept of Islam

Islam derives from the same semitic root as the Hebrew word Shalom, which means peace. Islam means "entering into a condition of peace and security with God, through allegiance or surrender to him". Prophet Muhammad received his revelations over 23 years from the angel Gabriel, who relayed the word of God. It was not entirely new but is the third great monotheistic religion. In Muslim eyes, Prophet Muhammad completes a succession of prophets, including Abraham, Moses and Jesus, each of whom refined and restated the message of God. The Qur'an, therefore, corroborates, updates and expands the Old and New Testaments. We can develop a deep theological understanding of the Islamic faith by reading the writings of scholars.

For the devout Muslims, Islam is a way of life. Its tenets and rules permeate almost everything, often including politics and government. In a world swayed by a misunderstanding of cultural differences, Islam and its adherents often are stereotyped and caricatured, branded with the violent or sexist image of a small minority of zealots. Central to Islam is the absolute sense that there can only be one God – Allah – and that he is the source of all creation and disposer of all lives and events. Hence, there is no God but God, and Prophet Muhammad is his messenger.

All people should become a single ummah – a community witnessing that fact. On the day of judgment, all will rise from the dead and go to heaven or hell. The Qur'an contains many moral exhortations, forming the basis of Islamic (sharia) law. It lays down generosity and fairness and the requirements for daily prayer, almsgiving, abstinence during daylight hours in Ramadan, and pilgrimage to Mecca. For Muslims, religion is an entire way of life, and one's faith and belief can guide every action or decision.

Shar'iah is the divine law of Islam by which Muslims should live their lives. It embraces every aspect of life, including family relations, inheritance, taxation, purification, and prayer, and it observes no distinction between secular and religious law. How far modern Islamic states follow this principle depends on the degree of secularisation they permit. Scholars explain that for many Muslims, prayer helps them intimately experience God. The 13th-century Persian Sufi poet Rumi spoke of his worship experience as a "delight" that opened the "window" of his soul.

Islam's emphasis on moderation

Islam emphasises moderation and balance in all matters related to faith, religious practices and social responsibilities. This universal principle permeated the holy Qur'an: "And God has not laid upon you any hardship in matters of religion" (Q 22:78).. God intends for you ease. The Qur'an reads: "God intends for you ease and does not intend for you hardship." (Q 2:185) The Qur'an reinforces this message again: "God does not burden a soul beyond its capacity." (Q 2:286)

A unique feature of the Qur'an is that while it spells out an ethical code, a moral path, a political system, a social norm, an economic order and a legal philosophy, it also presents in the life of Prophet Mohammad the practical exposition of the theoretical models contained in it. The Qur'an has not untouched hardly any aspect of life. Similarly, the Prophet's life penetrates every domain of human life with remarkable public and private versatility. This striking parallelism between the message of the Qur'an and the life of Prophet Muhammad indicates that it was to illustrate beyond doubt for every follower of the Qur'an that the pattern of life enunciated in the holy book remains universal. This unique dynamic of Islam has made it a distinctive faith.

The Prophet was, in fact, a human incarnation of the Qur'an. For what we find a wonderful philosophy in the static words of the Qur'an, we have a dynamic living counterpart in the life of Prophet Muhammad. The Prophet once told his close companion Abdullah ibn Amr: "Have I heard right that you fast every day and stand in prayer all night?" Abdullah replied: "Yes, O Messenger of God." The Prophet said: "Do not do that. Fast, as well as eat and drink. Stand in prayer, as well as sleep. It is because your body has a right upon you, your eyes have a right upon you, your wife has a right upon you, and your guest has a right upon you." (Al-Bukhari, 127)

While urging his followers to prepare themselves for life hereafter, the Prophet also admonished them to perform the necessary functions an individual is called upon to live a proper life. The Prophet believed that an ideal life had the right combination of essential elements: one that could enable him to lead a proper and contented life on earth, the other that could provide salvation.

It is an unfortunate irony that extremism is often associated with Islam when moderation is one of the most fundamental aspects of the

Muslim creed. Allah Almighty says: "Thus We made you a "wasat" (moderate) nation, that you might be a witness for all of humanity, and the messenger a witness over yourselves." (Qur'an, 2:143) The Arabic word "wasat" has several meanings. It implies being just, balanced, moderate, and the best. Islam is easily a haven of moderation. This trait has captivated many people to leave the confines of their faiths to other faiths to embrace I slam.

Muslims understand that God wants them to lead a balanced and moderate life so that they may serve as a "witness" or model for the rest of humanity. So what, exactly, does moderation in Islam mean? A Muslim's spiritual journey to God requires work at both the physical and spiritual levels. Thus, one should tend to increase in action with increased spiritual knowledge. The subsequent acts of worship have become much easier because they now have an increased faith and love for God rather than a sense of obligation and duty alone.

Moderation and balance are the best things in behaviour and attitude toward others. A true Muslim is a dignified person, but they are humble. a Muslim is not boastful, arrogant, or vainglorious. The Qur'an elaborates on this commandment:" And walk not on the earth exultant. Lo! thou canst not rend the world, nor canst thou stretch to the height of the mountains." (Q17:37)

The epic saying of the Prophet

The essence of his message is in his well-known saying: "Do for this world as if thou were to live a thousand years and for the next as if thou were to die tomorrow."

The Prophet stated:

"For a prudent person, he must have some moments;
Moments when he should commune with God,
Moments when he should be reflecting on the mysteries of creation,
And also moments spared for the acquisition of the money."

In other words, a faithful servant of God must apportion his time so that a part communicates with God through prayers. A part of it focuses on self-auditing oneself and reflecting on the mysteries of creation by seeking knowledge of the various secrets in nature and acquiring the necessary money to achieve one's needs. The Qur'an spells out a life which is a harmonious blend of the otherworldly and mundane aspects. The attempts that both these aspects of life are so organically related that one gives meaning and content to the other.

The Qur'an recognises two essential obligations of an individual: one to God and the other to society. Islam disapproves of asceticism and a life of self-denial. The Qur'an also disapproves of the lifestyles extreme – luxurious and pleasure-seeking. It calls for moderation in all activities to achieve a fuller life. The Prophet was efficient in his approach and guidance to his companions.

The advice of the Prophet

Once, the Prophet saw a wretched, ugly man with torn clothes. He asked the man the reason for his tragic state. The man replied: "O Messenger of God, I prefer giving all in charity, contenting myself with this shabby dress." The Prophet disapproved: "Not like that; God likes to see the traces of his benefit on his slave!"

The Qur'an forbids: "O children of Adam! Wear your beautiful apparel at every time and place of prayer, eat and drink, but waste not by excess, for Allah loves not wasters. Say: 'Who has forbidden the beautiful gifts of Allah which He has produced for His servants and the things clean and pure which He has provided for sustenance." (Q7:31-32)

It is the human preference for riches that the Qur'an cautions against and encourages us to maintain a balance between extravagance and parsimony. It recognises human nature, which has the dual impulses of compassion and an inherent love of wealth. In this way, Islam's religious teachings counsel temperance and prudence. In contrast, Islam's spiritual teachings urge selflessness and generosity.

The balance between the body and spirit, personal and civic responsibilities, and spirituality and the mundane affairs of life is a beautiful guidance bequeathed by Islam to humanity. The Qur'an further explains that a perfect model of religion does not lie in the mere performance of the rituals. It also has to consider the duties incumbent on an individual in his relationship with the community from which he draws sustenance.

We must remember that traditional scholarship emerged from the labours of scholars who lived a life of hermits over several decades, hibernating in mosques and caves away from the daily mart of economic and social strife. Pontification may be easy, but we must ensure we are not blurring the wafer-thin line that demarcates faith and heresy.

Reformation of feminist approaches

What Muslims certainly don't need are lazy calls from non-muslims for an Islamic reformation, the repetition of which merely illustrates how simplistic and hollo;w are some of the West's commentators on this issue. They find it easier to reduce the complex issue to a series of slogans, clichés, and buzzwords rather than attempt to examine the root causes or historical trends of the present crisis engulfing Islam. Several scholars feel that unless we recognise the importance of the socio-historical context of the Qur'an, our reading and understanding will not be able to guide us in our objective.

The process of reformation has to be gradual. It cannot be seismic and aggressively expansive, as most radicals tend to assume. In several Islamic reform movements, we are encouraged to be sensitive to the apprehensions and misgivings of the ulemas who have always been keen to protect their turf and constituencies. Social change flows from individual and collective efforts. In several cases, revolutionary movements have sprung from smaller beginnings. Lots of progress can come from more minor advances. Thousands of lesser improvements that build upon one another can represent an enormous societal advance. The soundest and best way forward is through innumerable small steps that could be just nudges and tiny pushes. We should wait for windows of opportunity to push significant changes through during these small steps. The first rule of learning is to do it in small chunks and through occasional big pushes when the momentum is strong. Brief bursts are better than one prolonged blast. Slower and smaller steps also help build up people's adaptability to changes. We should look for small innovations, not just blockbusters. By changing what they do, people move societies in new directions. Big, simple solutions are tempting but full of risks. For most outsiders, most of the time, the soundest and the best way forward is through innumerable small steps.

It is unfair to label the entire clerical community as obscurantist. If there are regressive elements among the clerics, there are also heretical minds among the modernists. Modernists cannot usurp the umpireship of the game. We need a level playing field where the clerical and libertarian fraternities appreciate and appraise each other with a spirit of genuine inquiry. However, the chasm between classicists and modernists is containable through a strategic rapprochement.

Imam Ghazali is on record saying that once he opened the doors of doubts, he could not close them. His firm resolve not to allow these doubts to contaminate his faith. Endowed that we have limited vision and cognitive abilities and cannot comprehend the complexities of the world and its vast mysteries, we must realise that we cannot keep continually speculating about many aspects of divinity. Despite being an intellectual colossus, ibn Rushd (known in the Western world as Averroes) acknowledged his work: "God knows every single letter, and perhaps God will accept my excuse and forgive my stumbling in his bounty, generosity, munificence and excellence—there is no god but He!"

Many theologians are strong proponents of *ijtehad* (the process of arriving at new interpretations of Islamic law through critical reasoning), the process of arriving at new interpretations of Islamic law through critical reasoning rather than mindlessly following the precedents of past scholars. In the early centuries of Islam, the process of *ijtehad* was an essential contributor to shaping Islamic law.

The truth of Islam

To observant Muslims, ritual prayer is as natural as sleeping or eating. Islam is not just one component of its believers' lives; it is a set of beliefs remembered on special occasions. Instead, for the devout, it is a way of life. Its tenets and rules permeate almost a vast gamut of activities, including politics and government. In a world swayed by misunderstanding of cultural differences, Islam and its adherents often are stereotyped and caricatured, branded with the violent or sexist image of a small minority of zealots.

Over millennia, the religion took form with the early Jewish prophets, underwent significant modification through Jesus and attained complete evolution through the divine revelations and their implementation at the hands of Prophet Muhammad, the final prophet. Among the Prophet's most pivotal tacts was rejecting the old Jewish concept of a "chosen people." Instead, he taught that all people are born Muslim and that anyone – regardless of colour, nationality or social standing – can join the Muslim community simply by submitting to God and reciting the words known as the shahadah: "There is no deity but Allah (God), and Muhammad is his messenger." Because of its powerful, cross-cultural appeal, Islam has won the hearts and minds of an estimated 1.2 billion people worldwide, making it the second-largest religion. Christianity has about 2 billion adherents; Hinduism is the third largest, with about 800 million. Despite its association across the world, about 85 per cent of Islam's faithful are not Arabs. South Asia has the largest Muslim population, with 275 million believers.

In contrast to moderation, extremism in any form is considered abnormal human behaviour, that is, being too liberal or too harsh in understanding. This behaviour is not in line with normative Islam. Neither of these approaches significantly hurt the image of Islam in its way. The Prophet said: "I fast but not every day, I pray at night but not all night, and I am a married man; whoever does not wish to follow my way, he is not from me." (Al-Bukhari and Muslim,143.) The Prophet often warned his companions against extremism and always advocated moderation. He always chose the easiest when given two choices, so long as it did not transgress the rules of Islam.

Sectarianism among Muslims

Muslim society has many strains of sectarianism with a diversity of hues and stripes—Sunni, Shiite, Barelvi, Deobandi, Ahmadi, and Mahdi Muslims—all of whom consider each other *kafirs* (non-muslims). Most of the leading lights of these sects lack familiarity with the complex field of Islamic political history and, hence, do not have the tools for grappling with the modern challenges confronting Islam.

Religiosity is good as long as it does not retard the organic evolution of a thought and belief system. Traditionalists and modernists must enlarge the prism through which they view each other. It will create accommodation for both while clarifying their respective perspectives. The world is now too complex, too interconnected, and too globalised to be divided into 'black' and 'white': 'the abode of Islam and 'the abode of unbelief'. The overall message is to break the monolith wherever it comes from. The fundamentalists must realise that their blind literalism could lead them to follow the letter of the law but betray the intents of foundational texts. We must not forget that the *shari'ah* (Islamic code) was for man and not man for the *shari'ah*.

The theme of moderation has been the leitmotif in Islamic literature since the time of the Prophet. The application of moderation covers all aspects of our worldly and otherworldly lives. The Qur'ān and the Prophetic traditions amplify the various injunctions in this regard.

The truth is that Islam has already had its reformation of sorts, in the sense of stripping of cultural accretions and a process of supposed "purification". Wasn't reform what precisely Muhammad ibn Abdul Wahab, the mid-18th century itinerant preacher, offered to the masses? He provided an austere Islam cleansed of what he believed to be innovations, which eschewed centuries of mainstream scholarship and commentary and rejected the authority of the traditional ulema or religious authorities.

Islam has already undergone a reformation

Islam is not only changing but is a force for change. Profound homegrown change is underway beyond the stereotype. The change is towards democratic gender equality and developing a vibrant civil society. This change relies on an unequivocally moderate, tolerant and open outlook drawing inspiration from the sources of Islam. The battle underway to reclaim the soul of Islam is challenging the conventions of tradition and unpicking the issues that have been at the heart of the revivalist agenda for decades: The call for an Islamic state and the reintroduction of the *shari'ah* law.

But the Muslim world is not a job lot. In each country, the nature of activism and its outcomes result from the particular and different circumstances of history and national experience. Malaysia's attempt to generate a new "civic Islam" is an exemplary and replicable example. By changing their relationship with traditional Muslims, they are recasting the potential of their future.

The Qur'an is the authoritative guide to proper living, along with tradition, called the hadith, based on the sayings and practices of Prophet Muhammad. Muslims view life as a test, says Sulayman S. Nyang, an expert on Islam at Howard University. It is a person's responsibility to live as closely as possible by the words of Allah in preparation for a "Day of Judgment", much like the one in which Christians believe. Muslims say the world someday will be destroyed and the dead resurrected, judged and sent to heaven or hell. However, sinners may take heart because, according to the Islamic council's handbook, the infinite mercy of God is eis in the Qur'anic statement that those who have even a mustard seed's weight of belief in God will eventually enter Heaven. Islam also teaches that each person has a direct relationship with God and that no intermediary is needed. As a result, Islam has no priests or other clergy.

We may find evidence of change in some fledgling endeavours that have still not found roots and any significant followers. However, their diversity and widespread distribution provide a necessary balance to a view of Islam and Muslims that is a result of the ideas of the Middle East and old Islamophobic stereotypes. It, however, should not make us defeat our worldview of Islam. Islam has attracted both Muslims and non-Muslims by the stellar achievements and the contribution of Muslims who have been instrumental in rolling out several unique initiatives,

It would be folly to suggest that terrorism fuelled by perverse interpretations of Islam doesn't exist. There is agreement on minor distortions in interpretative Islam, but terrorism cannot thrive on the foundation established on these minor di; distortions, but it is rooted in different ideologies. It would be naive to argue that the conditions that make such ideology seductive do not exist. But the most significant error would be to base our response to the extremism of the few on false propositions and an assumption that the Muslim world offers optimism.

When the Qur'an and sunnah (the traditions and sayings of the Prophet Muhammad) did not explicitly address an issue, or when there were conflicting statements from the Prophet Muhammad, a qualified legal scholar could use independent reasoning to come up with a solution. *ijtihad* was a vibrant legal process until the end of the tenth century,

Around this time, influential orthodox Sunni ulema (Muslim clergy with several years of training) began to argue against the process of independent reasoning, claiming that it could distort Islam. Instead, they advocated a literal reading of religious texts. Reformers resisted, warning that a rigid interpretation of *shari'ah* can be profoundly unhelpful in answering contemporary questions. But over the centuries, the literalists gained ground, leading to what some have referred to as a "closing of the gates of *ijtehad*". With this development, the intellectual and political decline was soon evident. The reasoning and logic which stood as the foundation of several Islamic traditions were shunned, not just by the fanatics but by the vast majority of Muslims. The most regressive doctrines took an unassailable hold on Muslim minds.

Consequently, the reforms that took place in the early years of Islam are progressive, changing with the needs of society. It was no coincidence that Islamic civilization led the world because of its ingenuity. However, the more detailed rules that the classical jurists laid out allowed many pre-Islamic customs to continue and reflected the existing society's needs, customs, and expectations instead of continuing the progressive reform set rolling during the prophet's time. The reform trajectory began at the time of the prophet and was thus halted in the medieval period through selective codification in the nineteenth and twentieth centuries. It marked the sunset of Islam's golden age. Invaders from North Africa pillaged the pluralism of Muslim Spain. Much of the Islamic empire slumped into a bottomless abyss from Cordoba to Baghdad. Out of 135 schools of Sunni thought, just four survived. The gates of *ijtehad had* narrowed and, in some places, closed, legitimising rigid readings of the Qur'an. To this day, Muslims still struggle with the idea of fostering independent thought.

Moderation needs to be comprehensive

Muslim women and men are called upon to exercise moderation in all aspects of their religious life. The Prophet confirms the essence of the Qur'ān's message: "Make things easy, do not make them difficult." (*Bukhari*) One commonly cited example is easing travellers' fasting obligation during Ramadhan to caution believers against excess. Such Islamic provisions have guided most Islamic scholars to understand the Qur'ānic quotation describing the Muslims as the "community of moderation". We are repeatedly encouraged to follow the Middle Path and shun extreme alternatives.

Islam instructs its followers to believe in this world and the world to come in such a way as not to overpower the one over the other. The Muslim has the right to enjoy this world's pleasures as it belongs to him. "But seek the abode of the Hereafter in that which Allah hath given thee and neglect not thy portion of the world, and be thou kind even as Allah hath been kind to thee, and seek not corruption in the earth; lo! Allah loveth not corruptors" (28:77).

During the first Islamic century, two interpretations of religious practice sprang up: *ahl al-ʿazīma*, which interpreted religious practices (as reflected in *shari'ah* rules, precepts and injunctions) and applied them strictly (to the letter of the law) without benefiting from exemptions under specific circumstances; and *ahl ar-rukhaṣ*, which considered, apart from these factors, the need for flexibility vis-à-vis the social context of the day, not to mention instances of need (*hāja*) and necessity (*darūra*).

Over the centuries, most Islamic scholars and Muslims worldwide (whether Sunni or Shia, irrespective of legal school) have preached and followed the path of moderation in religion. While strictly devoted to fundamental principles (such as the content of the creed, or *aqīda*, including five prayers a day and fasting in Ramadhan, and prohibitions such as avoiding alcohol and pork), they have adapted to changing times (for example, integrating aspects of new cultures, producing legal opinions for the latest scientific or technological challenges, and so on).

The golden mean

In a way, the Qur'ān reiterates the Greek ideal of "the golden mean" and "nothing in excess". Over-indulgence in worldly pleasures is discouraged because it leads to several mental and physical perversions. Man is inclined to feel a spiritual vacuum if he has not tempered his earthly life with the needs of his soul. Similarly, asceticism, which verges to the point of harshness, deprives him of experiencing the subliminal beauty of life, which is one of God's great bounties. In short, we can have a more balanced individuality if we harmonise our worldly and spiritual needs. A unique feature of the Qur'ān is that while it spells out an ethical code, a moral path, a political system, a social norm, economic order, and legal philosophy, it also presents in the life of Prophet Muhammad, the practical exposition of the ideal model it expounds.

This striking parallelism between the message of the Qur'ān and the life of Prophet Muhammad demonstrates that his life was a role model for every follower of the Qur'ān that the pattern of life enunciated in the Qur'ān is capable of being practised by every individual. For what we find a wonderful philosophy in the static words of the Qur'ān, we have a dynamic living counterpart in the life of Prophet Muhammad.

For the Qur'ān, Propet Muhammad was an individual through whom every word shone like a gleaming star. The Qur'ān was the focal object of Islamic virtues and the life of the Prophet, a mirror that reflected in the purest form the impressions of the Book. As the Qur'ān says, "O Prophet! Lo: We have sent thee as a witness and a bringer of good tidings and a warner. And as a summoner unto Allah by His permission, and, as a lamp that giveth light." (33:45-46 perhaps tis philosophy has been made most famous for its mention in al-Nawawī's renowned collection of forty hadith, the Prophet Muhammad said, "Be in the world as though you were a stranger or a wayfarer." (122-3, Hadith 40). This hadith has also ben recorded in Nukhaaari:

On the authority of Abdullah ibn Umar (ra), who said:

The Messenger of Allah (saw) took me by the shoulder and said,

"Be in this world as though you were a stranger or a wayfarer."

And Ibn Umar (ra) used to say,

"In the evening do not expect [to live until] the morning, and in the morning do not expect [to live until] the evening. Take [advantage of] your health before times of sickness, and [take advantage of] your life before your death."

[Bukhari]

The Qur'ān spells out a life that is a harmonious blend of the otherworldly and mundane. It emphasises that a perfect model of religious life is not one based on the mere performance of rituals. One must also integrate oneself with the family and the community. Synthesis is an attempt to give meaning and content to one another. The Qur'ān recognises two essential obligations of an individual: one to God and the other to society, thereby ruling out any possibilities for a life of asceticism and monasticism.

The Qur'ān also disapproves of the other extreme of lifestyle – materialistic and pleasure-seeking. It calls for moderation in all spheres to achieve a complete and wholesome life. The Prophet himself was realistic in his approach. Once, the Prophet saw a wretched, ugly man with torn clothes. He asked the man the reason for his tragic state. The man replied, "O Messenger of God, prefer giving all in charity, contenting myself with this shabby dress." The Prophet disapproved: "Not like that; God likes to see the traces of his benefit on his slave!"

Moderaation–the quintessence of Islam

Moderation is a fundamental and distinguishing feature of Islam. God says, "We have made you a nation justly balanced." (2:143) Additionally, when the Qur'ānic verse, "As to monasticism which they invented, We did not prescribe any of it for them" (57: 27) was revealed, the Prophet Muhammad commented, "Do not overburden yourselves, lest you perish. People [before you] overburdened themselves and perished. Their remains are found in hermitages and monasteries," (*Musnad* of Abu Ya'la). In other words, excesses may eventually develop into significant thickets of problems and even become a threat to the well-being and security of the Muslim community.

The middle way describes the divergence between attachment and aversion, being and non-being, form and emptiness, free will and determinism, hedonism and asceticism, and harsh self-denial and sensual pleasure-seeking. To use the words of Socrates, "Remember that there is nothing stable in human affairs; therefore, avoid undue elation in prosperity or undue depression in adversity."

It isn't about endurance, nor is it about apathy. It's about balance. Michael Singer explains it well in *The Untethered Soul*. He writes, "The more you work with balance, the more you can sail through life. All forces are in harmony."

During the early Makkan period, "Al-Yusraa," or "The Easy Way", was used to describe Islam. There is a plethora of verses that testify to the Qur'ān's underlying philosophy of moderation.

- "Truly with hardship comes ease." (94: 6)

- "God will assuredly appoint, after difficulty, easiness." (65:7)

- "Whoso fears God; God will appoint for him, of His command, easiness." (65:4)

- "We shall speak to him, of our command, easiness." (18:88)

- "God desires to lighten things for you, for the human being has been created weak." (4:28)

- Here is a sampling of hadiths that amplify the Qur'ānic verses.

The Prophet Muhammad once asked a companion, "(Is it true) that you fast all day and stand in prayer all night?" The companion replied that the report was indeed accurate. The Prophet then said: "Do not do that! Observe the fast sometimes and also leave (it) at other times. Stand up for prayer at night and also sleep at night. Your body has a right over you, your eyes have a right over you, and your wife has a right over you." (Sahih Al Bukhari, Volume 7, Hadith 127). The Prophet Muhammad said, "Do good deeds properly, sincerely and moderately. Always adopt a middle, moderate, regular course to reach your target (of paradise)." (Sahih Al-Bukhari, Vol 8, Hadith 470)

"The good deeds of any person will not make him enter Paradise (i.e., no one enters Paradise only through his good deeds)." The Prophet's companions asked, "Not even you?" The Prophet replied, "Not even myself unless God bestows His favour and mercy on me. So be moderate in your religious deeds and do your best. None of you should wish for death, for if he is a doer of good, he may increase his good deeds, and if he is an evildoer, he may repent to God." (Sahih al-Bukhari, Volume 7, Hadith 577)

The Prophet once told his close companion Abdullah ibn Amr, "Have I heard right that you fast every day and stand in prayer all night?" Abdullah replied, "Yes, O Messenger of God." The Prophet said, "Do not do that. Fast, as well as eat and drink. Stand in prayer, as well as sleep. It is because your body has a right upon you, your eyes have a right upon you, your wife has a right upon you, and your guest has a right upon you." (Al-Bukhari, 127)

Abu Hurairah reported that the Prophet said, "The religion (of Islam) is easy, and whoever makes the religion a rigour, it will overpower him. So, follow a middle course (in worship); if you can't do this, do something near to it and give glad tidings and seek help (of Allah) at morn and dusk and some part of the night."(Al-Bukhari-Riyad as-Salihin, Book 1, Hadith 145)

The Prophet believed an ideal life had the right combination of essential worldly and spiritual elements. One could provide dignified life on earth; the other could give salvation to him in the hereafter. The essence of his is in his well-known saying, "Do for this world as if thou were to live a thousand years and for the next as if thou were to die tomorrow." (Jamius-Saghir, II/12, Hadith No:1201)

The Prophet advised: "O children of Adam! Wear your beautiful apparel at every time and place of prayer, eat and drink, but waste not by excess, for Allah loves not wasters. Say: 'Who has forbidden the beautiful gifts of Allah which He has produced for His servants and the things clean and pure which He has provided for sustenance." (7:31-32)

The Qur'ān encourages us to maintain a balance between extravagance and parsimony. It recognises human nature, which has the dual impulses of compassion and an inherent love of wealth. In this way, Islam's religious teachings counsel temperance and prudence, whereas Islam's spiritual teachings urge selflessness and generosity.

Distractions from the path of righteousness could include even family, "Wealth and sons are the ornaments of the nearer life, but enduring works of righteousness are better before your Lord…." (18:46) In another passage, the Qur'ān appears to contradict it, "O you who believe, do not forbid the good things that God has allowed you," (5:87). Still, the passage goes on to say, "nor go to extremes, for God does not love those who go to extremes." Their righteousness was to be always with them as a source of balance and harmony, part of their everyday life. They were to be "In the world, not of the world."

✻ ✻ ✻ ✻ ✻

2. HOW MODERN, MODERATE MADRASAS ARE DRAWING GLOBAL ACCLAIM

As the evening prayer ended, hundreds of boys rushed out of the building in waves, mats slung over their shoulders. On opposite sides of a dusty road, thousands of Muslim students in this remote farming town prepare for different futures.

On one side, inside a traditional Islamic seminary, teenage boys in skullcaps study ancient texts to become imams. On the other hand, students are hunched before computers in college classrooms, learning to become doctors, pharmacists, and engineers. The distance between them is about 50 feet, but it could be five centuries. In the middle is a bearded Muslim cleric. These students attend India's many Islamic boarding schools or madrasas. Contrary to popular belief, several teach secular subjects like science, medicine, technology, social sciences, history, classical Islamic texts, and vocational courses in agriculture and mechanics.

But their reputation has taken a battering in recent decades, thanks to a wave of extremism. The image of madrasas suffered on account of the searing and strident critiques. In secular countries, the State has not only denounced them but attempted to wrest exclusive control over them. However, the negative stereotypes we get to read in sections of the media do not present the actual picture. The majority of madrasas present an opportunity, not a threat. For young village kids, it may be their only path to literacy. For many orphans and the rural impoverished, madrasas provide essential social services: education and lodging for children who otherwise could well find themselves the victims of forced labour, sex trafficking or other abuse.

Islam had once become a major, even obsessive, topic of public debate over the past two Madrasas. The religious schools that educate millions of students in the Muslim world were once held responsible for all sorts of ills. Critics have denounced them as dens of terror, hatcheries for suicide bombers, and repositories of medievalism. Muslims have now primarily recoiled from the violence and sweeping anti-Westernism that was at one time unleashed in their name.

Madrasas no longer retained the cutting-edge educational philosophy. There has never been a sincere attempt to galvanise and reinvigorate these seminaries. The most significant change was the shift from imparting knowledge of ma'aqulat (rational sciences) to rote learning and interpretation of manqlat (received religious texts). Rather than undermining the madrasa system, policymakers should engage it. Beards and bombast may make for good newspaper copy. Still, the reality of the madrasa system is far different: they give the impression that they are leading a revolution in orthodoxy and diversity, but at the same time, they are hosting a quiet debate about reform. Madrasas largely maintain cold neutrality to avoid getting trampled in the policy brawl. This approach has steered them through several controversial debates. Madrasas need a new orientation to address the contemporary generation's growing challenges. Scholars have devoted much thought to making them relevant to changing times.

The revolutionary role of madrasas

Madrasas have played an essential role in the history of Islamic civilisation. They have been powerful nodes in the learning system and precursors of several revolutionary achievements in fields as diverse as jurisprudence, philosophy, astronomy, science, religion, literature and medicine. It was only when the Golden Age of Islam began to decline that the madrasas lost their academic and intellectual purity and ceded prime space to Western-oriented education.

The spread of madrasas played a vital role in consolidating doctrinal positions and legal thinking, which now form the dominant position among Sunnis. In time, the Shias developed their religious seminaries, called hawzas, which play a similar role. Some of the most famous madrasas are the Deoband in India, al-Azhar in Egypt, Hawzas of Qum in Iran and the Zaytunia in Tunisia.

From the 18th century, large parts of the Muslim world engaged with modernity in its colonial form – an encounter that transformed almost all aspects of Muslim societies. Modern schools, higher education institutions, new official languages, and a new epistemology set their roots. Madrasas continued to provide religious instructions, though they underwent remarkable transformations in form, teaching and, to some extent, content.

The First War of Indian Independence of 1857 divided the composite madrasa education into secular and religious spaces. This division emerged in the Deoband and Aligarh traditions, where Sir Syed Ahmed Khan emphasised the development of an educational system according to the needs of the time while Deoband insisted on preserving religious values and tradition in the Indian subcontinent. The social composition of madrasas began to change, becoming less affluent and more rural, with the more inspirational Muslims joining Western educational streams. The madrasas lost intellectual vitality, and the teaching became pedantic, with little creative, mental or intellectual development scope. Every project these seminaries undertake needs a lot of in-depth research and scouting and hunting for suitable teams comprising appropriate peer groups. It can introduce various subjects and themes that can synergise into higher and advanced learning levels.

While the debate over the modernisation of madrasas continues, several madrasas are taking steps to initiate change to bring them in tune with modern times. Several madrasas in India are open to non-Muslims and teach secular subjects as well. In Gujarat, Maharashtra and Uttar Pradesh, among several other states, madrasas provide modern education through computers and the internet. Some have allowed the entry of Muslim girls, and ones like Moin-ul-Islam near Agra have a large number of Hindu students on roll and have even introduced Sanskrit as a subject.

The modernist Islamic seminaries

The reformists of *madrasa* education insist that knowledge in Islam is one whole and that the division between *dini* (religious) and *duniyavi* (worldly) knowledge—with the two opposed to each other and which many contemporary *ulema* seem to have accepted—has no sanction in the Qu'ran. The Qu'ran repeatedly encourages believers to ponder the mysteries of creation as signs of God's power and mercy. In the entire scripture, there are about 600 verses directly commanding the believers to reflect, ponder, and analyse God's magnificence in nature, plants, stars, and the solar system, and far from leading to doubt and disbelief, scientific investigation—if conducted within properly defined Islamic bounds—can deepen one's faith in Islam.

But *madrasas* are not immune to change and have embarked on a campaign to hybridise their indigenous courses with modern curricula. Many of them are trying to forge a Muslim identity that is compatible with contemporary culture and resistant to the blandishments of radicalisation. Likewise, few *ulema* could claim to be completely satisfied with the *madrasas* as they exist today. Indeed, leading *ulema* are themselves conscious of the need for change in the system.

Critics often charge the madrasa system with anachronism, citing its insistence on the supreme pedagogical value of the old texts. The traditionalists argue that, apart from connecting students to the canonical tradition, the "Nizami curriculum" enhances the students' mastery of every discipline and enables scholars to solve any contemporary problem.

But one of the most accomplished modern products of madrasas, who had a very close association with the Deoband seminary, Ebrahim Moosa, who studied at India's leading Islamic seminary, avers: "Few have been able to refute the charge that the texts used are redundant and at times impenetrable, save to a few scholars who have spent their lives mastering them. Indeed, most texts are frustratingly terse, forcing teachers and students to scour commentaries and super-commentaries for help."

He further argues: "For decades, critics have petitioned for more lucid texts. But inertia has turned the texts and syllabus into inviolable monuments to the past. The result is that students are impoverishedly prepared and lack the confidence to engage the tradition critically to meet the needs of a changing world. At its worst, the system recycles intellectual mediocrity as righteousness."

The issue of reforms is, however, quite complex. The adoption of state-led modernisation has a complex interplay of several factors such as trust, financial incentives, the impact of state-led policies on the functioning of madrasas and its implications on the community resources which the madrasas are now accessing for their finances, and, course the faultiness within Islam that are deep;y ingrained in the various strains of Islamic thought that permeated the faith. Islam is not a monolith, and madrasas owe allegiance to diverse schools of thought which are hybridising into further new strains. The government's understanding and strategy for dealing with madrasas must evolve from a black-and-white perception to a more wholesome one.

Policymakers need to be more sensitive to the sentiments of Islamic clerics, and efforts are required to combat anti-Muslim" debates. The deep reservations of madrasa managers about the government are all not ill-founded, and several of the duplicitous actions and policies of the state give enough ground for a creeping scepticism.

We should attempt to make new madrasas and universities patterned on ancient Samarkand or Bokhara. Rather than stressing only madrasa modernisation, let us take madrasas centuries back in history to their glorious traditions of the Islamic Golden Age. That may be more successful in winning the hearts and minds of the custodians of madrasas. The al-Azhar University in Cairo, the oldest and most significant of all the madrasas, was the Mediterranean's most sophisticated school during the early Middle Ages. We should strive to make these new madrasas religious seminaries and universities like al-Azhar. Indeed, the very idea of a university in the modern sense – a place where students congregate to study various subjects under eminent scholars – is generally regarded as an innovation first developed at al-Azhar.

The goal of modern madrasa endeavours must always be to highlight and share fresh ideas. The aim must be to cover a diverse set of perspectives. Efforts to stay "politically correct" have contributed to an absence of structured debate and discussion on how best to make modern education accessible to millions of impoverished Muslim youth so that they get jobs. The government's understanding and strategy for dealing with madrasas must evolve from a black-and-white perception to a more wholesome one. Debates on "secular versus non-secular" and "pro-Hindu versus anti-Muslim" should be discouraged. Thus, apart from equipping madrasas with tools of modern education, we have to orient the mindset of students to attune it to social realities and sensitise madrasa students to emerging socio-cultural paradigms. It must be the fundamental objective of the modernisation process if we want madrasas to be relevant to our times.

Most of these Islamic schools present an opportunity, not a threat. For young village children, these schools may be their only path to literacy. These provide essential social services for many orphans and the impoverished who are struggling. They continue to serve parts of developing societies that Governments never reach. For parents mired in poverty and forced to work long hours with limited breaks, *madrasas* are vital for ensuring their children are supervised, fed and taught to read and write.

As their graduates go out and take up a range of new careers and as pressures from within the community as well as from the State and the media for reform grow, these Islamic schools, too, are changing. Far from typifying one end of the polarising spectrum of traditional versus modern and religious versus secular education, the State must continue to use Islamic seminaries as part of the regular educational paradigm. It must evolve an educational grid that allows constant movement between *madrasas* and mainstream educational institutions.

A need for modernist madrasas

Policymakers must pay closer attention to the seamless transition from *madrasas* to mainstream education. The State should not interfere in religious instruction, which should be the business of private individuals and associations. Second, regular inspections should ensure the orientation of learning of Muslim communities to their traditions. The gap between pro-democratic rhetoric and reality continues to widen.

The consensus is that *madrasas* can bring both secular and religious education. Since the students are undergoing learning in classical and modern science and secular and religious thought, they should be able to spot scriptural distortions better. They also tend to be more connected to their communities and the mainstream society. Their stable sense of identity, both religious and otherwise, shields them from radicalism. The *madrasas* are allies in India's fight against extremism.

Some recent reform efforts have focused on modernising the teachings. It includes adding computer proficiency and English language classes to strengthen the employment potential for *madrasa* students.

However, the introduction of computer skills at many *Deoband-type madrasas* is focused only on equipping them with functional literacy and not enabling them to engage with the modern technological revolution.

Thus, apart from equipping *madrasas* with tools of modern education, we have to orient the mindset of students to attune it to social realities and sensitise them towards emerging socio-cultural paradigms. It must be the fundamental objective of the modernisation process of *madrasas*. The efforts to stay "politically correct" have contributed to an absence of structured debate and discussion on how to make modern education accessible to millions of impoverished Muslim youth so that they get jobs. We must remember that cultural isolation would only lead to stagnation. The *madrasas* betray a more profound dissatisfaction and fatigue with a redundant learning system.

Shibli Nu'mani, a renowned twentieth-century scholar from within the madrasa circles, noted: "For us Muslims, mere English (modern) education is insufficient, nor does the old Arabic *madrasa* education suffice. Our ailment requires a compound panacea. One portion eastern and the other western."

While it is true that most *madrasas* have outlived their role, the syllabuses can be updated to make them meaningfully relevant in the modern context. They need a makeover and bolstering of their learning patterns with more intelligent thought processes. Teaching and learning should follow a path that respects traditional sensibilities and attempts to synergise both classical and modern knowledge.

Some modern progressive seminaries have turned a new leaf, and many more are modernising. Students who remain unfamiliar and underinformed about the intricacies of their faith can be transformed in a negative direction by arguments that seem to impair their mindset and call for *jehad* when the debates and discussions on Quranic verses go out of context. However, students from these new-generation religious schools are grounded in classical and liberal values.

Adopting modern techniques for learning

There is a need to deploy a significant pedagogical shift in the importance of mastering foundational concepts before progressing. This philosophy has become a bedrock of the approach even in ordinary institutions. If you just let people have a strong foundation, the next few come pretty easy, and no learner has gaps in understanding.

The potential of technology is because it augments, and not replaces, the invaluable human element in education. Muslim institutions envision a future where tools are potent allies to educators, enabling them to tailor instruction to each student's needs. Artificial Intelligence is a revolutionary evolution in modern technology.

The initial scepticism about artificial intelligence (AI) in education is dispelled mainly by the capabilities of some components that demonstrate the ability to answer complex questions and accurately generate explanations and additional queries. This leap in AI technology can revolutionize how students interact with educational content.

The implications of AI in education extend beyond individualized learning; they promise to reshape classroom dynamics and teacher-student interactions. Several Muslim institutions have initiated integrating AI in regular learning to enable real-time feedback and tailored instruction, which presents a paradigm shift in educational practices. It promises a future where every student can access a personal tutor and get valuable insights and tools to address each learner's unique needs by providing personalized guidance and fostering a deeper engagement with the subject content and material.

New vision for madrasas

The right approach would be to temper classical and traditional learning with liberal thought. It can foster a culture that will engender the two learning streams to nourish each other. It will enable the students of these seminaries to lead lives that are as true to their faith as attuned to modern needs. It will build them into empowered stakeholders who will shape their future and those of their communities.

An enlightened and productive human capital is society's most precious asset, and *madrasas* can undoubtedly be key enablers in this task. Modern subjects can also help students gain a good grounding in secular subjects and technical skills so they do not lose out in an increasingly competitive and globalised workplace.

Madrasas need to keep pace with the imperatives of changing times. They should enlarge their worldview and have enough resilience and malleability to respond to the fluid and changing world. We must remember that cultural isolation would only lead to stagnation. The madrasas betray a more profound dissatisfaction and fatigue with a redundant learning system. In these seminaries, leadership and inclusion are everyone's responsibilities. We must keep gender and empathy at the heart of our institutional philosophy. We must be a force of change for good and take our responsibility with pride and privilege. Madrasas have the potential to influence Muslim children's development positively, allow pupils to explore and understand their own identity and strengthen community cohesion. However, they suffer setbacks due to impoverished teaching standards and narrow curricula. Our wish should be to unlock ourselves further from academic rigidity and allow current social and other critical realities to challenge old dogma.

Madrasas should be locomotives with a strong sense of purpose, passion, perseverance, and a partnering approach in supporting an environment that can change students' lives. Madrasas should also focus on hiring the best teachers and providing them with a unique learning ecosystem to mould students' destinies. They should be passionate about transforming the landscape of social and educational change. There is an unnecessary and disproportionate focus on purely theocratic studies, which needs decoupling to give space to modern studies. Students who are unfamiliar with the intricacies of their faith can be sullied d by arguments that seem to call for *jehad* when taken out of context. However, students from these new-generation Islamic schools are grounded in classical and liberal values. We must persuade ourselves to face the current realistic infeasibility of the academic approach. It can help neuter the academic incapabilities of students, who get polarized when they move out to the real world.

Since madrasas typically have financial crunches, they should funnel their scarce resources into enhancing the quality of teaching. They should not squander their precious and scarce resources to set up impressive facades that unnecessarily consume huge costs without adding any additional and worthwhile value to the institution. This model is increasingly essential because funds are shrinking even with compromised donors. A fair part of the budget must equip good libraries to expose students to informed writing and analysis. Though madrasas may have to make a hard decision, they must renounce donors with a vested agenda. It can insulate the madrasas from being driven by donors who may use the madrasa platform to promote their ideologies. It will also prevent students from being trapped in non-academic activities. Most madrasas' future is not sure because of a lack of funds. The upcoming times will be challenging, and very few madrasas may attain the milestones they have been able to achieve the milestones they recorded all these decades. However, if their impact and outcomes remain appealing, enough funders will gladly provide ongoing support.

The way forward

Madrasas have a noble history of being used to further the cause of science and learning in medieval Islam. Still, that tradition has vanished because of a relatively uneducated theological establishment taking over the administration of most madrasas. Madrasa students learning science would locate themselves at the borderlines of natural sciences and faith as a practice. The fusion results in something like opening the mind towards newer developments and turning an open and enlightened mind towards the sacred. This would generate a balanced and refined personality who can negotiate between differences of approach and stand as a bridge between Islam and modernity.

Students who tend to come out of these seminaries are better connected not just to their communities but to mainstream society, and their stable sense of identity, religious and otherwise, shields them from radicalism. They are allies in India's fight against extremismMost madrasas have a segregated female wing imparting a similar syllabus of education. Several new endeavours at modern madrasas have facilitated the development of nuanced and in-depth insights into various facets of society, including gendered norms, which give insights into women's capabilities and vulnerabilities. It has also helped scale up interactions at multiple levels in the community, enhancing understanding of the diverse activities in madrasa learning.

* * * * *

3. REDISCOVERING ISLAM

"These callous and fanatic murders have nothing to do with us," say the mullahs." This has nothing to do with Islam," call out the imams. "Islam means peace," wail the worshippers. These disclaimers and variations on them have been repeated countless times by Muslim commentators. They are ripostes to distance people from guilt by association with those Muslims who have performed a sinful action in the name of Islam." Muslims are subversive jihadists. The Middle East is perpetually unstable." And "Islam has bloody borders." If you've already decided, you'll find a way to twist the facts to support your conclusion. And if the facts don't work, you can always hire new ones. There's a simple enough reason for this: Islamophobia has become an industry. In the absence of alternative narratives which can make sense of Muslim extremism, place it into context and guide American domestic and foreign policy, we get stuck with the voices we have. Too often, these have been unqualified and uninformed.

The essential message of historical and contemporary decrees is clear: the self-appointed guardians of Islam need to be revered, not cross-examined or put under a scrutiny lens. The rules handed down and already conjured have become established; precedents must be accepted and followed, not interrogated. The pronouncements of imams and sheikhs, mullahs and ayatollahs – whether educated or semi-literate – are God's word and will—several times, such issues involve the application of basic understanding and not any specialised knowledge.

Despite what these religious despots would have their followers think, Islamic history is full of free thinkers who have stood up to such authoritarianism. During the 8th century CE, when sharia law was getting its final shape, the Persian writer and thinker Ibn al-Muqaffa declared that it could be used as a political tool by kings and clerics manipulating the rough and credulous. During the 9th and 10th centuries, many writers, satirists and free thinkers joined him in denouncing dogmatism. It is true that.

Muslims require home-grown imams who understand Islamic philosophy correctly and can provide context for Muslims to lead their lives. But these imams must also be trained to have intellectual rigour, to be able to challenge and be challenged and to engage in the debate, which too often takes place outside the mosque gates. However, better religious leadership is only part of the solution. Muslims must individually focus on what the Prophet Muhammad called the "greater *jehad*", the inward struggle for holiness and submission. Central to this is re-engaging with the Qur'an.

Rediscovering the Qur'an

Every Muslim will tell you the Qur'an is an eternal scripture. It is timeless, and its words remain unchanged. The Qur'an itself says:" And if all the trees on earth were pens and the ocean (were ink), with seven seas behind it to add to its (supply), yet would not the words of Allah be exhausted (in writing): for Allah is Exalted in Power, full of Wisdom" (Q31:27). We call it Holy Qur'an, Noble Qur'an, Glorious Qur'an, Al-Furqaan, Al-Kitaab, Al-Zikr, Al-Noor, Al-Huda.

To Muslims, the sacredness of the Qur'an is expressed even in their relationship to its physical presence. Islamic teaching spells out that Muslims must not touch the Qur'an without first undergoing a ritual hand-washing called *ghusl,* which places them in a state of ritual purity. Most homes have wrapped The Qur'an in a specially stitched satin or velvet cover. The entire Qur'an extends over thirty primers called a juz.

All of this is taking place in the Muslim world and among Muslims, but also in Western lands, where a growing number of Muslims are contributing to the scientific debate and defining a new significance of the Qur'an as a text diffused worldwide by scholars who have recently contributed and are taking a keen interest in the dialogue on varied facets of the Qur'an and offering further reflection. They can go a step further and consider, along with their scholarship and vision, the perspective of the past approaches and the impact of such interpretations in the contemporary world.

These debates are producing several questions. What is the significance of interpreting the Qur'an for Muslims worldwide and in religious studies? How could/should a (new) interpretation of the Qur'an be functional to the development of future societies? We studied the Qur'an with the aid of several classical and contemporary commentaries under the guidance of a cleric. During my academic career, I attended innumerable conferences and met many people who argued about the meanings of sacred texts. The more I learned about the Qur'an and engaged with it, the more intense my struggle became. The more I learnt about Muslims' intellectual history and thought about the differences and distinctions, as well as similarities, between classical and modern scholars, the more I had to struggle with what Muslims throughout their history have made of Islam.

We must realize that the meaning and context of words and phrases of the language in which the manuscript has undergone translation can be more accessible if we know the cultural history that may or may not be totally in sync with the Qur'anic setting. For example, when the Qur'an chides the kaafir (non-believer)r, this can be translated as "infidel," "one who rejects faith," or simply "disbeliever" – to mention some of the standard translations of the word. Each translation implies something significantly different and depends on how English speakers understand these words and their historical baggage.

Reformation in Islam

Islam is changing. But if you want to notice this change, you have to turn your gaze away from the threat of terrorism, Islamophobic nightmares and the erosion of democratic foundations. Islamophobia promotes a "racialised view of Islam" – the actions of the few represent the "intentions" of the whole. Islamophobia promotes a racialised view of Islam, viewing Arabs, Middle Easterners and Muslims generally as one interchangeable, subversive, homogenous mass; the actions of the few represent the intentions and aspirations of the whole. Thus, we believe a plausible connection between bin Laden and Saddam could exist. The resulting costs in American lives, treasure, and credibility are hard to quantify. It is Islamophobia's fruit: poisonous policies.

Islam has changed radically, and the roots of democracy are soon germinating and growing into vibrant shoots. More and more Muslims, with better literacy and education than their grandparents often had, are returning to the primary texts and chipping at the cultural layers that have accumulated over the years. However, specific and severe aberrations continue to persist. Saudi Arabia's governing structures are being centralized, remoulded, and reined in. Its religious doctrine is no longer firmly committed to the teachings of Muhammad ibn Abd al-Wahhab. The trend began a few years ago, and even before the present ruler became the crown prince, it started accelerating. The Saudi governance system has undergone rapid and radical restructuring with far-reaching changes since its foundation is a combination of procedural shifts, personnel changes, bureaucratic restructurings, and changes in jurisdiction that are revolutionizing the role of Islam in the Saudi state—and public life.

However, for all the potentially radical, cumulative effects, most of these changes are technical adjustments, redistributions of duties, or changes in appointment patterns. Rhetoric and tone also shift in ways that suggest more radical moves could come at some point. There have been some suggestions of marginalizing but no frontal assault on Wahhabi teachings; long-standing structures have survived and are immune and adapting to existential challenges, at least for now. There is no total dismantling, but changes are taking place incrementally. The structures are undergoing remoulding but not abolition. Even as Saudi religious institutions change, their tools are evolving, ostensibly for increasing governing efficiency but primarily for political agenda.

The truth is that the vast majority of Muslims in the world are not Arab, Arabic-speaking or located in the Middle East. In places like Indonesia, Malaysia, Pakistan, Morocco and Turkey, a homegrown change is effected by the determination to adress poverty, underdevelopment, and lack of genuine, effective popular democracy, which has been the general condition of Muslim existence. It is, of course, easy to lecture the voiceless when you are in a position of privilege, but that gives no one the right to speak on behalf of people one doesn't even live with. Sadly enough, though, some of the people lecturing the Muslim community today are the very same ones who've been sitting in positions of power for decades without having proven their added value either to the country or the community they pretend to represent.

Let's stop manipulating secularism and let the principal become again a constitutional right for granting freedom of religion, equality among citizens and protection from government interference. Let's stop questioning the national identity of Muslims to demonise them as eternal "others" – inherently hostile aliens and impossible to integrate. Let's stop misinformed speakers from commenting on Islam and Muslims, and find a platform in the media.

Principles of Islam

These principles rest on the Qur'an, sunnah, and *ijma,* which means consensus of people and qiyas(analogical reasoning). Each school was known as a madhhab in Arabic, and there were slightly differing views, for example, on inheritance, private prayers, and public worship. All four were, nonetheless, acceptable to Sunnis. A school tends to dominate an area: Hanifi in what would be the Ottoman and Mughal Empires, Maliki in North Africa, Ash-Shafe'i in lower Egypt, east Africa, southern Arabia and South East Asia, Hanbalis in Saudi Arabia (where the Wahabis of Najd followed the principles of Ibn Taymiyah,1263–1328, a follower of Hanbal). However, two or more schools co-exist in large cities like Cairo. However, the active part of the lives of the Imams spans a short century; their work, along with the corpus of traditions and hadith(sayings—and doings—of the Prophet, his traditions), to a large extent, moulded Islamic civilization and dominated its intellectual activity. The five schools of thought generally agree that Islamic laws (1) change with time and with the change of place or circumstance; (2) must avoid harm; (3) may be discarded if they have a cause ('lilah) which itself has disappeared, and (4) must serve the common weal ("public maslaha").

There is a provision of *ijtehad*(the process of arriving at new interpretations of Islamic law through critical reasoning) in Islam which allows consideration of the latest developments and realities, and leading Muslim scholars can guide us on how to deal with them. The vast and silent majority of Muslims neither follow Wahabi nor Shia beliefs; hence, their wishes must be taken into account when choosing a panel of Muslim scholars *Itehad* requires effort and serious thought; it is always tempting to take the easy option and fall back on historical interpretations and the opinions of ancient jurists. Muslims tend to see classical authors in rather romantic terms: perfect individuals, incapable of making a wrong judgment. Classical scholars themselves are also guilty of perpetuating this. They have revered taqlid, or blind people, the following of predecessors to such an extent that it has now become a sacred principle. During the Abbasid period, the so-called 'Golden Age of Islam' from the 8th to the 13th century, the classical scholars decided to 'close the gates of *ijtehad*'.

They were concerned with multiple interpretations of Islam that increased during that period. In particular, they wanted to stop the abuse of *ijtehad* by people who were not theologically or legally qualified. In Muslim society, theologians could discover significant solutions through recourse to the literature comprising scriptural insights and their application to specific contexts. It was, therefore, conceived that we could similarly address the difficulties resulting from modern challenges by using analogical reasoning rooted in existing methods. It could effectively enable the achievement of a similar objective in developing viable solutions. This approach could be disseminated on a broader scale, facilitating a more extensive buy-in from various stakeholders. The freezing and the closure of the tools of *ijtehad* appear to have had devastating consequences for the evolution of revolutionary Muslim thought and philosophy. The degeneration of the interpretative approach of Muslims led to stagnation. It impeded the intriguing development process of ijtehad, further hindered by repressive forces, leading to its closure of *ijtehad*. What remained were standardized practices, which eventually became final.

Approach of modernists

Most modernists believe that the concept of *ijtehad* could respond to relevant contexts with necessary modifications to meet the challenges of the coming times. *Ijtehad*, in the sense of interpretation and reasoning based on sacred texts, should provide a contemporary solution for the troubles besetting Muslim societies, including the status of women, relations between Islamic sects, the role of Muslims in non-Muslim societies, dealings with non-Muslims in Islamic states, economic and social injunctions in Islamic doctrine and related issues.

In the past, the doctrine of *ijtehad* didn't find favour with the repressive ruling establishments in Islamic states, and it was used for different reasons by religious leaders. The thrust worldwide towards more democratic dispensations and the vastly enhanced freedom of expression provided a more friendly climate for the revival and development of *ijtehad*. While the absence of compulsion in religion is a well-known moral precept of the Qur'an, its impact and impetus seem to have escaped most of this breed. If they are religious, it is only because the veneer of faith gives them even more authority to intervene and interject, condemn and condone the actions of all sorts of any number of other people.

The iconoclastic strain they initiated has been a powerful engine in Islamic discourse, expressing strong criticism either of the stagnation of scholarly institutions and religious practices postdating the early Muslim generations or of those institutions and practices themselves. It has characterized the eighteenth-century revival and reform movements and crystallized in the modern reformist movement. Since it desacralised the ulema, it was stridently opposed by the traditionalists who still endorsed servile conformity to the Ulema. It is time to clearly understand the pristine message of the Qur'an rather than reading it with the eye of its medieval-era jurists, scholars and ideologues. There is an urgent need to understand the core message of Islam that remains buried under layers of medieval interpretation.

The great scholars picked up the strands from the epic works of intellectual colossuses and polymaths such as Al-Farabi (872-951 AD), Al-Ghazali (1058-1111 AD), Ibn Rushd (1126-1198 AD), Ibn Arabi (1165-1240 AD), Ibn Khaldun (1332-1406 AD). Much of the work of eclectic scholars had already lost their autonomy by self-seeking despots who portrayed themselves as sentinels of everything that constituted Islam. The vast reservoir of exegetical guesswork had already been exhausted. The new intellectuals, riding on the cusp of a new wave of enlightenment, mesmerized and influenced the Muslim minds. Most of them tried to resurrect the hallowed scholarly tradition of the great reformist thinkers of the Golden Age.

Among those who laid the foundations for the reformist ideology and hermeneutical approach to Qur'an were Jamal al-Din al-Afghani, (d.1897), Muhammad Abduh (1849 –1905)), Shah Wali Allah (1703-1762), Hassan al Banna (1906–1949) Sayyid Qutb (1906–(1966) Rashid Rida (1865–1935) Mohammed al Ghazali (1917–1996) Muhammad Iqbal1877–1938)Abul A'la Maududi (1903–1979) Mohammed Arkoun (1928–2010) Ali Shari'ati (d.1977) Yusuf al-Qaradawi, (1926-) Ubaid Allah Sindhi (1872-1944).

Damage from fruitless debates

For those known nowadays as Islamists or fundamentalists, the failures and shortcomings of modern Islamic lands have become an encroaching menace that looms large across their horizons. They fell away from authentic Islam and lost their former greatness. Those known as modernists or reformers take the opposite view, seeing the cause of this loss not in the abandonment but in the retention of old ways and the inflexibility and ubiquity of the Islamic clergy, who, they say, are responsible for the persistence of beliefs and practices that might have been creative and progressive a thousand years ago but are leading downhill today. Modernists' usual tactic is not to denounce religion as such, still less Islam in particular, but to direct their criticism against fanaticism. It is to fanaticism—and more particularly, fanatical religious authorities—that they attribute the stifling of the once great Islamic scientific movement and, more generally, of the freedom of thought and expression.

If Prophet Muhammad's life were revolutionary, its aftermath would have seen a monotonous recital of hadiths(sayings—and doings—of the Prophet, his traditions) and inflexible analyses of Qur'anic verses, where historical context is taken up or ignored to suit the interpreter. Memories of early Islam have hardened into dogma, and many scholars have taken the hadiths (sayings—and doings—of the Prophet, his traditions) very fastidiously as seriously as tablets of stone and made them override the Qur'an. Hadiths(sayings—and doings—of the Prophet, his traditions) have to be appropriately aligned so that we weed out those that contradict the core Qur'anic injunctions.

We can no longer afford to turn Islam into an arena for fruitless debates where the mountain goes into labour and finally produces just a mouse. There have been brave liberalists who have been intelligent critics of the polemics of the ulema but ended up becoming labelled as heretics and pawns of the Western scholarship whose intentions have not necessarily been well-intentioned. We cannot allow pseudo-scholars masquerading as saviours of Islam to keep stoking the fires of intemperance.

The world is now too complex, too interconnected, and too globalised to be divided into 'black' and 'white': 'the abode of Islam' and 'the abode of unbelief'. The overall message is to break the monolith wherever it comes from. The fundamentalists must realize that their blind literalism could lead them to follow the letter of the law but betray the intents of foundational texts. The future of freedom in the Islamic civilization lies in the unique insights that modern discourses have provided – that the *shari'ah* was for man and not man for the *shari'ah*. Luckily, the sources that will help nurture that insight are more abundant in Islamic theology and jurisprudence than what is perceived.

Alfaz-O-Maani Mein Tafawat Nahin Lekin
Mullah Ki Azan Aur, Mujahid Ki Azan Aur
Parwaz Hai Dono Ki Issi Aik Faza Mein
Kargas Ka Jahan Aur Hai, Shaheen Ka Jahan Aur

(There is not a speck of difference in words and meanings
Bu the clarion call of a muezzin and Mujahid are poles apart
The vulture and falcon soar in the same skies
But the world of falcon is far, far different from that of vulture)
– Iqbal

A need for a fresh outlook

There have been consistent attempts to make the ulema see the need for a non-clerical perspective in formulating an Islamic response to the changing complexities and multiple transitions in a fast-evolving world. Hopelessness cannot become permanent, and we must address forces driving the new ideological tides. Islamic liberalism must be authentic and well-intentioned to find conviction with the ordinary Muslims who are essential stakeholders in the evolution of Muslim thought and practices. Otherwise, it will remain a manufactured discourse of the West with whom several liberalists share kinship ties. Meeting real Muslims pushes aside the media narrative that is so pernicious and harmful. Why? Because much of what Islamophobia peddles is hyperbolic, fanciful, or meaningless.

Modernists should be well-equipped with classical and modern scholarship tools. Otherwise, it will lead to intellectual anarchy. It takes a new generation to produce an original thinker. Most others are just pale reflections burnishing their credentials by recycling the existing scholarship. It is not that Islam did not have great thinkers from the ranks of the ulema. The real problem is that the ummah(Islamic humanity) lacked the creative and intellectual talents to grasp the vastness of their erudition. True, the ulema have repeatedly churned out scholarships suited to their ideology, compromising the scholarship principles. In all matters of religious scholarship, purity and morality of the conscience is a critical tenet. It is not paradoxical that most leading modernist scholars are products of Islamic seminaries and not elite Western institutions.

The process of reformation has to be gradual; it cannot be seismic and explosive, as most radicalists tend to believe. There are several layers to Islamic thought, and each has to be understood before we rediscover its new roots. Radical thinking is fraught with significant hazards and requires great caution. Any opinion has to be dispassionate and objective, formulated through what Edmund Burke, the great British parliamentarian, popularly defined as the cold neutrality of an impartial judge. Sadly, several Islamic reform movements have suffered account of ulterior motives, and hence, protagonists of all such initiatives should appreciate the apprehensions and misgivings of the ulemas.

Dangers of radical outlook

Radical thinking can be a dreadful and hazardous enterprise and lead society into a moral abyss unless certain fundamental caveats check them. New contours have to evolve within a tightly disciplined Islamic framework. The traditional principles of rigidly regulated analyses and interpretations do not stand on quicksand; it has resulted from centuries of labour of highly committed and pious scholars, the byproducts of whose works have morphed into several Western disciplines. Several hardliners within the clerical ranks have impeded and constrained the course of the reformist debate. But these hardliners have also checked the tide of anarchic impulses among a large section of intemperate scholars whose sacrilegious hyperbole does not reflect erudition.

We must remember that traditional scholarship emerged from the labours of scholars who lived a life of hermits over several decades, hibernating away from the daily economic and social strife to work on the new frontiers of Islamic thought single-mindedly. Pontification may be easy, but we must ensure we are not blurring the wafer-thin line that demarcates faith and heresy. Too many puzzlements impact Islamic scholarship. It is still in a fluid state primarily because the traditionalists are still grappling with the perplexing tools in the arsenal of Western critics.

The interaction between Western and Islamic thought is not too old, and setting a gold standard would be premature. There are too many variables in the jigsaw puzzle of Islamic reforms. We must guard against the army of ill-intentioned Western cohorts masquerading as Islamic scholars. By taking any radical stand, we cannot easily rubbish a tradition of scholarship built through centuries of perseverance and assiduity by highly eminent men, many of whom were polymaths. Much of Western scholarship of today owes a great deal to the works of Ibn Sina, Ibn Rushd and Ibn Khaldun.

Role of hardliners

Hardliners have their unique place in all discourses, and their presence helps tame unchecked and anarchic impulses. The most sage advice for the marquee thinkers and promoters of new paradigms is: No matter who you are, how experienced you are, and how knowledgeable you think you are, always delay judgment. Give others the privilege to explain themselves. What you see may not be the reality. Never conclude for others. We should never focus only on the surface and judge others without understanding them. Building a new paradigm of thought isn't as easy as most naïve and self-proclaimed reformers believe. One cannot assume the authority to decide what is obsolete, antiquated, and worn out. It is the collective conscience that will always override the individual conscience. It is equally valid that clerical confabulations have acquired more and more opacity as the forces of modernity continue to make inroads into their imagined utopian enclaves.

Suppose we want to develop Islamic thought in a way that suits the needs and concerns of contemporary Muslim society. In that case, bold reforms will be required, particularly closing the ever-widening gap between the Islamic disciplines and the daily challenges of Muslims. Part of this approach requires questioning and then finding solutions to the thickets of problems of Islamic thought created over the past several hundred years in the post-formative period of Islam. Notions such as mutability and immutability, religious versus irreligious, and sacred versus profane may need further exploration. Many approaches to Islamic disciplines that were not sacred in the formative period have since become sacred. Yet the calls for reinterpretation have been rejected by the conservative ulama, who regard themselves as the 'guardians' of Islam. Those with the courage to take such a bold step are often labelled as heretics, aiming to subvert Islamic tradition.

Modernists will need a massive effort to replace the existing scholarship. Modern Islamic scholarship has not matured enough to propound theories that stand the scrutiny of both classical scholarship and the current Renaissance. We can still not confidently say that modernists have all the answers to Islam's challenges. The process initiated by thinkers like Muhammad Abduh and Fazlur Rahman may have moved out of nascence but has still not gained legitimacy. Many of their ideas are stillborn and will need time to establish themselves. The road ahead lies not in stubbornness or arrogance but in a reasoned dialogue between all stakeholders singularly driven with the purpose of human welfare within a rigid Islamic framework.

Conflict between traditionalists and modernists

It is unfair to varnish the entire ulemic (clerical) community with the same brush of obscurantism. If there are regressive elements among the ulema, there are also heretical minds among the modernists. Modernists cannot usurp the umpireship of the game. We need a level playing field where both embrace each other with a respectful acknowledgement of frailties and foibles in their fraternities. The search for truth will allow the clear light and enable civilization to grow rich with the insights of these seekers. Several strands in the traditionalist thought bristle with flashes of liberalism, and the greening effect will soon grow vibrant. Ulemic thought is no longer monochromatic; hybridization is fast catching up and is metamorphosing into variegated scenic beauty. Keeping this grandeur, the dull strands of modernist discourse will develop bright shoots in the nourishing soil. Nature is already bridging the islands inhabited by illustrious luminaries of liberal values, which is the cherished achievement of the Enlightenment and has converged them into a confluence of iconoclastic philosophy.

Muslim thinkers lost their mo;orings and faced difficult times. We are living in a problematic world, tolerating dogmatic ideologies and allowing the debates to degenerate into an onslaught on the very foundations of the Islamic faith. The ulema has a right to be cautious when the voices of liberalism emanate only from the Westernized elite. It is unfair to blame ill motives on the ulema, blackening them with accusations of obscurantism when they may be critically pursuing reason and truth. Those infusing reformist impulses carry the most authentic and credible batons for igniting and reigniting modernist notions from within Islamic theocracy. They are the ones who are hollowing out the decaying layers of Islamic theology. It is straightforward to sermonize from the lofty pedestals of chairs established by Western universities, protected by the immunities and privileges that go with these positions. Many of them have to remain understandably accountable to their patrons. There is no reason to believe that an unpalatable opinion for Islamic renewal dominates the entire clerical spectrum and bandwidth. There have been highly creative and talented individuals, even within the clerical ranks. Neither traditionalists nor modernists have anointed spheres, nor are they mutually exclusivist, but they are fed and sustained by each other.

Role of ijtehad

Modernists have repeatedly called for unconditional *ijtehad* or independent judgment of scriptures. Iqbal defined *ijtehad* as exerting a view to forming an independent judgment but not being independent of the *Qur'an* and *Sunnah*. He opposed freedom of thought, which makes man deviate from Divine guidance, but endorsed the independence of *ijtehad* to fight rigidity and stagnation. Iqbal mentioned two consequences of the release of *ijtehad* claimed by modern Muslim movements: their revolt against the finality of the schools and their firm stand on the right of private judgment. When discussing the freedom of *ijtehad* or independent review, Iqbal did not regard any independent assessment as *ijtehad*. Instead, he believed that those with the knowledge must exercise it and whose character can be entirely relied upon. In his emphasis on the qualifications of exercising *ijtehad*, Iqbal explained in his *Reconstruction of Religious Thought in Islam*, "It is the duty of the leaders of the world of Islam today to understand the real meaning of what has happened in Europe, and then to move forward with self-control and a clear insight into the ultimate aims of Islam as a social policy" Then, Iqbal suggested specific qualifications as follows;

1. Knowledge of Islam and deep understanding of the ultimate aims of its ideology, institutions and politics.

2. Understanding of the modern problems that beset the Muslim world.

3. Closeness to the Prophet's way and understanding of his methods and approach.

4. Reliable moral character so that decisions could gain legitimacy.

Since there is an acute shortage of such specialists qualified to exercise *ijtehad*, Iqbal observed that a committee of people, including Islamic scholars, should be formed and those with good knowledge of contemporary problems and possessing true Islamic character. Through their combined efforts, they will be able to contribute to the reconstruction of Islamic law and fulfil an essential need of society.

The democratization of the public space for debates has caused aorate dome ous. They must stop fulmination against each other by cherry-picking verses and then quote quetery. There is now an increasing trend of expansion of the tribe of pseudo-scholars with half-baked ideas of Islam and actively patronized by the media.

Legitimate space for all opinions

Liberals must continue to seek accommodation with tradition and faith as they have done in the past. Plural societies, though, can be built by interrogating our long-cherished practices and withstanding the winds of either heresy or obscurantism. Religiosity is good as long as it does not retard the organic evolution of a thought and belief system. Both the traditionalists and modernists must enlarge the prism through which they view each other; this will create accommodation for both of them while strengthening their respective constituencies. Islam is an expansive and living religion. It has moved with the currents of history, and its billion-plus practitioners bring a broad spectrum of interpretations and beliefs. Within a generation, his successors – the caliphs – controlled territory stretching from the Atlantic to the Indus Valley. It was not just an astonishing feat of world conquest, comparable to the accomplishments of Alexander and the Caesars: it had religious and social implications as far-reaching as the death of Christ and the Bolshevik Revolution. While Christianity merely revitalized the ancient Roman Empire, providing it with a new legitimacy which enabled it to overcome the crises posed by nationalism and barbarian invasion, Islam created a brand new polity – in effect, the world's first ideological state.

Better religious leadership is only part of the solution. Muslims must individually focus on what the Prophet Muhammad called the "greater *jehad*", the inward struggle for holiness and submission. Central to this is re-engaging with the Qur'an. There is no spiritual hierarchy in Islam, as all Muslims are equal in the eyes of God. Still, a group of self-defined "scholars" of varying quality has emerged over the centuries and assumed Islamic theology's academic leadership. They have been allowed by ordinary Muslims to legitimize their monopoly on interpreting the holy book. There is a handful within the scholarly fraternity that encourages followers to question, reason, evaluate and reach informed conclusions for themselves. But these voices have too often been crowded out by more austere, confrontational and literalist ones.

One of the consequences is that there is a "male-dominated world of Qur'anic exegesis." Little wonder then that the "rampant misogyny of male Qur'anic exegetes," and not Islam itself, has demeaned the status of women in much of Muslim society. All this needs to change. While Islam provides us with substantial inner strength, much of the outward practice centres around communal worship based on brotherhood – and that aspect is becoming an increasing challenge. The Muslim faith has remained strong for many years, but it must guard itself against the growing disillusionment of many of the co-religionists.

Crystallisation of Islam

In a sense, the advent of Islam was a revolution that succeeded after long struggles, but only partially. After the Islamic conquests of the seventh century, there was a continuing tension between the new religion and its message and the ancient societies of the countries that the Muslims conquered. Islam came not into a new world, like Christendom in Europe, but to lands of ancient civilization and deep-rooted traditions. This tension between Islamic dynamism and the older spearheads of the river-valley societies continued through medieval into modern times. For example, Islamic doctrine is egalitarian; from the beginning, Islam denounced aristocratic privilege, rejected hierarchy, and adopted an environment of meritocracy.

Resistance to all these agendas was quite solid and aggressive. On the whole, Islam triumphed in certain limited spheres covering social and family life. Most political and public matters were overwhelmed by the ancient traditions of the regions, which survived in an Islamic disguise, notably in the persistence of the autocratic, monarchical form of government. Hence, through the centuries, history took a wrong turn fo;r Muslims and perverted Islam. The Islamic community was ruled by non-Muslims, bad Muslims, renegade Muslims, and those who had betrayed the heritage of the Prophet and were driving the community as a whole into the abyss of chaos.

The status of the *shari'ah* disciplines, be they ahadith al-fiqh (Islamic jurisprudence) or tafsir, does not seem particularly encouraging as far as any fu; fundamental changes to their existing paradigms are concerned. They lost their vitality and spark once the shari'ah disciplines were developed and matured in the fourth/tenth and fifth/eleventh centuries. Amateurish scholars rarely test the waters and challenge the existing paradigm without competitive preparation. The established order triumphed in the confrontation between tradition and the reassessment of that tradition. The methods developed by leading figures such as Bukhari (d. 256/870) and Muslim (d. 261/875) were considered the pinnacle of hadith (sayings—and doings—of the Prophet, his traditions criticism). The ulema did not feel a need for significant refinement or reinvestigation. Modern Western critical scholarship on hadith has, until recently, been largely ignored in the Muslim world because it questioned the authenticity of hadith and because of its methodology. There have been few attempts at rethinking varied aspects of ahadith within Islamic scholarship.

* * * * *

4. TIME TO LOOK INWARD

We now live in an age of baffling and multiple problems on almost all fronts, even as revolutionary developments in science and technology have redefined civilization and driven an enormous explosion of progress in diverse fields. Most of these problems defy human answers. Finding common ground can help us at a time when unified action is more crucial than ever. As a species, we must embrace the oneness of humanity as we face global issues like pandemics, economic crises and ecological disasters. There are many more critical issues (guns, terrorism, climate change, labour, immigration, globalization, infrastructure, defence, investment, taxation, healthcare, education, and research) that require the synergy of diverse intellectual forces –irrespective of their hues – to come out with valid answers and solutions. The Qur'an came to speak to all of humanity. However, it came to mean that it was not in a vacuum but within a historical context. Hence, its immediate objective was the moral and religious situation of the Arabs of the Prophet's time. Therefore, we must recognize that although we can always hear the Qur'an speaking anew to our particular case, the universal and timeless dimension cannot obscure the historical context.

Reappraisal of mindset

Islam originated in Saudi Arabia, the birthplace of its prophet, Muhammad. The culture of the place of origin has always shaped the Western image and understanding of Islam. The prism of history sees Islam through the perspective of events in the Middle East. Saudi Arabia's adherence to puritanical Wahhabism, with its insistence on a very narrow interpretation of *shari'ah* – Islamic law, is seen as indicative of the authentic norms of Islam. Through the science of explanation that has transformed many in every age and all Islamic languages, the Qur'an is kept alive as a force in the lives and cultures of Muslims everywhere. It remains relevant to every age through commentaries no longer limited to Arabic or other Islamic languages. Indeed, critical Qur'anic commentaries have appeared significantly in English and other European languages spoken by European Muslims. English, in particular, is fast becoming a significant Islamic language, and the Islamic literature in the English language has grown exponentially.

At no time in world civilization have we required a pure and authentic spiritual revolution, and tragically, we have been ignoring the power of spiritual values when they are needed most. It requires a pure intention, as well as great spiritual discernment, to repel the evil promptings that are sullying our culture and return to the source of all: the prime cause of all that exists, that "no human vision can encompass Him" (Q6:103) either physically or conceptually: and, therefore, "He is sublimely exalted above anything that men may devise by way of definition.' (Q16 : 1902)

Muslims need to realize that our first identity is the vicegerent of the Almighty, and their first allegiance is to the One God, their Nourisher and Sustainer. It is for God to revive the weakening spiritual currents, but Muslims are also responsible for reinforcing their faith. Faced with the challenge of modernity, many Muslims today, rather than accommodate themselves to the age-old fudges that have prevailed in so many Muslim societies, have resorted instead to a kind of textual Puritanism. Instead of referring to how things have taken place in colonial Morocco, Ottoman Turkey, or, much further back, under the Abbasid caliphs, they prefer to return to the 'simple truths' of the Qur'an.

The field of Qur'anic studies is currently in vogue among scholars. This proliferation of scholarship is taking place at a time when no consensus exists on a central core of works to define the field, let alone on a programme to train future scholars. Islam promotes and teaches humans to practice balance in all aspects of life with moderation. Humans are also influenced and shaped by their culture and traditions; political, economic and psychological experiences shape their attitudes and behaviours and separate and divide them. Consequently, their world views and religious views differ from place to place, era to era and across cultures, thereby continuing to irresponsibly link religion(in this case, Islam) to the oppression of women. The alleged retrograde practices of the community take the world's focus away from understanding the overwhelming problems of the Muslim world and the cause of its troubles. It provides an easy scapegoat for those looking to legitimize their illegitimate actions, which are detrimental to humanity.

Disconnect between theoretical and practical Islam

There is a legitimate disconnect between the application of Islamist tenets and the context of societies in which they have not been appropriately disseminated or understood. If we had to define Islamism, it would be motivated to pursue the Qur'ānic view of humanity in all aspects of life. One who serves humanity first prevents harm and protects society. At its very core, Islam prescribes the principles of justice and equity for peace and human development, as well as compassion for all humankind. The same root word of Islam is related to the word *salaam* (peace). Islam is a universal religion that speaks to humanity. In his last great address at Arafat, the Prophet summed up his philosophy by decrying barriers between people. Islam, for him, transcended divisions of caste, colour and race. "All mankind is from Adam and Eve, an Arab has no superiority over a non-Arab nor a non-Arab has any superiority over an Arab; also a white has no superiority over a black, nor a black has any superiority over white except by piety and good action."

Muslim admiration for Western civilisation

Islam is adrift in a sea of troubles and a deluge of disparate ideologies pedalled by contradictory ideologues. It continues to be beset by threats from classicists and modernists, apart from other sectarian conflicts. Compounding the misery is the growing deterioration of the Muslim character. Muslims are themselves to blame for their downfall. Islam is reluctant to enact a range of essential reforms. There was a time when they lived in a make-believe euphoria—singing paeans to their ancestry's grandeur and remarkable resilience. This rhetoric was gauzy and was undoubtedly superb. But the reality soon started dawning on them, and they must acknowledge that Western powers are bolstering their capabilities at an exponential pace. Dysfunctionality, corruption and arrogance paved the way for Western domination. The best response to Western overreach is for Islam to become the original version that enabled it to command supremacy over large swathes of world territories. Islam cannot forever forestall the need for reforms in the face of a modernizing, increasingly demanding society.

At first, the Muslim response to Western civilization was one of admiration and emulation—an immense respect for the achievements of the West and a desire to imitate and adopt them. This desire arose from a keen and growing awareness of the Islamic world's weakness, poverty, and backwardness compared with the advancing West. Muslim writers observed and described the West's wealth and power, science, technology and forms of government. The rise of a Western civilisation effectively quashed any lingering Muslim hope of resurrecting their lost sheen of glory for a time. The secret of Western success lay in two achievements: economic advancement, especially in industry, political institutions, and freedom. Several generations of reformers and modernizers tried to adapt these and introduce them to their own countries in the hope that they would thereby be able to achieve equality with the West and perhaps restore their lost superiority. In our own time, this mood of admiration and emulation has, among many Muslims, given way to one of hostility and rejection. This mood is primarily a result of humiliation that generated a feeling of despair and defeat—a growing awareness among the heirs of an old, proud, and long-dominant civilization of being overtaken, overborne, and overwhelmed by those they regarded as their inferiors.

The introduction of Western commercial, financial, and industrial methods brought great wealth. Still, it accrued to transplanted Westerners and members of Westernized minorities, and only a few among the mainstream Muslim population were fortunate to get a share. In time, these few became more numerous, but they remained isolated from the masses, differing from them even in their dress and style of life. For vast numbers of Middle Easterners, Western-style economic methods brought poverty, Western-style political institutions brought tyranny, and even Western-style warfare brought defeat.

It is hardly surprising that so many were willing to listen to the newly erupting voices telling them that the old Islamic ways were best and that their only salvation was to throw aside the pagan innovations of the reformers and return to the true path that God had prescribed for his people. These Islamists see Western practices and views regarding women as part of a Western cultural offensive which accompanies political and economic offensives. For many believers, western gender practices were more like aggression than liberation, and Islamist women can find some genuine advantages for themselves in their new interpretations of Islam. Muslims are in a tortuous situation and need to urgently work out ways of building a common identity. Islam needs to position itself better to navigate the global political headwinds. It must also solidify its religious policies and make them amenable to modern challenges.

Distortion of Islam

The distorted images of Islam stem partly from a lack of understanding of Islam among non-Muslims and partly from the failure of Muslims to explain themselves. The results are predictable: the hatred feeds on hatred. Ignorance of Islam exists both among Muslims and non-Muslims. Non-Muslims, ignorant and misunderstanding Islam, fear it. They believe it threatens their most fundamental values. Fantasy, conjecture and stereotypes replace fact and reality.

Similarly, Muslims have misconceptions. They, reacting to the hate and fear of non –Muslims, create a kind of defensive posture within their societies and a combative environment built on militant rhetoric. They decry whatever is Western as inimical to their existence. The voices of peace and tolerance have drowned in this heat and misunderstanding. We need sanity in all quarters to let the truth prevail. Let us allow the flowers of truth to bloom. That is the right approach.

The reforms that took place in the early years of Islam are progressive, changing with the needs of the society. However, the more detailed rules that the classical jurists laid out allowed many pre-Islamic customs to continue and also reflected the needs, customs and expectations of the society in which they lived instead of continuing the progressive reform that began during the time of the Prophet. The trajectory of reform started at the time of the Prophet. Thus, It was stopped in the medieval period by further elaborating fiqh: Islamic jurisprudence, which was then selectively codified in the nineteenth and twentieth centuries. The modern world is incredibly different from the early centuries of Islam and the medieval era. The example of progressive reform that took place in the early period of Islam must guide us in addressing the needs of the people today. Islam did provide superior justice for women, but the trajectory was checkmated.

Cultures that arose since then have been characterized by customs and local cultural leanings more than genuine Islamic values. The lives of the first Muslim women represent valuable models transcending time and physical boundaries. These Islamic models can serve as powerful, culturally authentic tools in advancing the human rights agenda towards increased female empowerment in Muslim societies and communities' political, social and economic spheres. The contributions of these women to the Muslim community are undeniable and may even appear almost mythical to some. Some may mistakenly subscribe to the erroneous notion that contemporary Muslim women cannot attain such great stature and that these are just tales of Muslim legends without modern-day applicability. The women represent many others who lived, fought, learned, worked and led during Islam's foundational period and beyond. Their male companions and the caliphs who assumed Muslim rule following the demise of Prophet Muhammad treated them with respect, admiration, and appreciation – and as equals.

One of the worst aspects of contemporary Muslim societies is the tendency of some Muslims to abrogate to themselves extraordinary wisdom and their insistence on having authority over Islam. They assume their interpretation is the only true and correct one, and everyone else must emulate them. It is like saying that there is only one way to be a Muslim; all other ways of being a Muslim are not only wrong but should be subjugated, leading the way to a totalitarian society.

A need for introspection

The colonial era has left deep scars and has blurred our sanity. While rejecting the West and criticizing it for the shortcomings of our world is seductive and an easy way to cast away the burden of our accountability, it doesn't absolve us. We remain transfixed with the image of the aggressor, the predator; it is part of the colonial legacy. But it is time to turn our gaze inwards. We must look at ourselves realistically and clinically; unless we acknowledge our liability and responsibility, we can't recover from the chaos in which we have fallen.

The postcolonialist Muslim debate on the structure, functions, and goals of Islam in the contemporary world is a complex debate whose participants are formulating contradictory assessments and plans for action, often reflecting their perspectives in tones of mutual hatred. What can unite these voices and views is a shared vision of Islam and the conviction that Islam is the only legitimate force of solidarity and cohesion in today's world and one that is now convincingly acknowledged as the only approach to overcome the traumatic experience of Western colonialism and its legacy.

Islam must galvanise itself and its adherents to combat the wrenching impact of alien forces whose influence in economic, political, and cultural permutations loom so supremely on Islam's cultural, political, social and economic horizons. Many religious thinkers believe in strengthening Islam through internal renewal (*tajdid*)without "suffering" modernity. They believe in accepting and fostering religious modernization by harmonizing with the indigenous culture. It, in turn, requires reinforcement and reformulation of the Qur'an's divinely legislated spiritual, political, social, and economic moral values to enable Muslims to heed and practice the modern call for equality, equity, and justice as proclaimed and exemplified in the Qur'an and *sunnah*. They feel that a pristine form of Islamic culture can undoubtedly eliminate and purge our civilization of the harmful effects of Westernization.

Many people have called for a reform of Islam, but the truth is that Islam needs to be rediscovered but not changed. The deeper one goes into Islamic scholarship, the more the harsh images of Islamic law as a vehicle for stonings and amputations fade away, and we will have a surprisingly sophisticated and progressive approach to faith that dates back to its earliest days. Muslims don't need to throw out their religion and create something new; they need to re-examine the original scriptures and find the original meanings as the Prophet, a man of progressive vision, would have seen them, even if his earliest followers did not always see as far.

Islamic jurisprudence

The wealth of *hadith* and the minutiae they address raise an important question: does the *hadith* mean that every action of Muslims is predetermined and fixed forever? The answer lies in the discourse between the Prophet and Muadh ibn Jabal, a *qadi* on his way to al-Yaman as judge.

Imam Tirmidhi and Imam Abu Dawood have both narrated that when the Prophet) sent Mu'adh ibn Jabal to Yemen (as a governor), he asked him:

"How will you judge if you are asked to do so?"

Mu'adh said: "I will judge according to the Book of Allah."

The Prophet: "And if you do not find it in the Book of Allah?"

Muadh: "Then I will judge according to the Sunnah of His Messenger."

The Prophet: "And if you do not find it in the Sunnah of the Messenger or the Book of Allah?"

Muadh: "Then I will exercise my opinion and not be negligent."

The Prophet then patted the chest of Mu'adh with his hands and said: "All praise is due to Allah, Who has guided the emissary of His Messenger towards that which He guided His Messenger." [Abu Dawood)

The Islamic principles, which encourage adaptability and rational choice based on *ijtehad*, independent judgment, shura, consultation, and ijma(meaning consensus of the people, are reflected in the exchange. Rationality and man's judgment play a part in arriving at decisions. *Ijtehad*is is the Islamic legal term meaning "independent reasoning," as opposed to taqlid (the following of It is one of four sources of Sunni law and is applied where the Qur'an and sunnah (the first two predecessors) sources) are silent. It requires a thorough knowledge of theology, revealed texts, and legal theory (usul al-fiqh-Islamic jurisprudence), as well as a sophisticated capacity for legal reasoning and a thorough understanding of Arabic. It is considered a required religious duty for those qualified to perform it. It should remain a source of guidance by using analogical reasoning (*qiyas*). According to many scholars, its results may not contradict the Qur'an. They may be discouraged in cases where the consensus of the people (ijma) is available. Sunnis believe *ijteha* is fallible since more than one interpretation of a legal issue is possible. Islamic reformers call for a revitalization of *ijtehad* in in the modern world.

Concept of Islamic law

What is the system of Islamic law? In his lifetime, the Prophet Muhammad was both the religious and the political leader of the community of Muslim believers. His revelation, the Qur'an, contained laws concerning ritual matters and inheritance. Still, it was not primarily a legal book and did not include a lengthy legal code found in parts of the Hebrew Bible. When the first generation of believers needed guidance on a subject not addressed by revelation, they went directly to Muhammad. He either answered of his own accord or, if unsure, awaited divine guidance in the form of a new revelation.

With the death of Muhammad, divine revelation to the Muslim community stopped. The role of the political-religious leader passed to a series of caliphs (Arabic for "substitute") who stood in the Prophet's stead. That left the caliph in a tricky position when resolving complex legal matters. The caliph possessed Muhammad's authority but not his access to revelation. It also left the community in something of a bind. How would the law be determined if the Qur'an did not speak clearly to a particular question?

The answer that developed over the first couple of centuries of Islam was that the knowledge of the Qur'an could improve by referencing the Prophet's life—his *sunnah*, his path. We can address such problems by reasoning and analogy from one situation to another. There was also the possibility that a communal consensus existed on what to do under particular circumstances, which had substantial weight.

This fourfold combination—the Qur'an, the path of the Prophet as captured in the collections of reports, analogical reasoning and consensus—amounted to a basis for a legal system. But who would be able to say how these four factors fit together? Indeed, who had the authority to say that these factors and not others formed the sources of the law? The first four caliphs, who knew the Prophet personally, might have been able to make this claim for themselves. However, after them, the caliphs were faced with a growing group of specialists who asserted that they could collectively ascertain the law from available sources. This self-appointed group came to be known as the scholars—and throughout a few generations, they got the caliphs to acknowledge them as the guardians of the law. They gained control over the legal system by interpreting a statute that originated with God. That made them, not the caliphs, into the heirs of the prophets.

Shariah is the body of Islamic law developed by religious scholars (*ulema*) after the death of the Prophet Muhammad. It provides moral and legal guidance to Muslims. *shari'ah* is a product of n the Qur'an and the *sunnah* (the recorded traditions or customs of the Prophet). The Qur'an has about 80 verses concerning legal issues, many of which refer to the role of women in society and to important family issues, such as marriage, divorce, and inheritance.

The importance of shar'iah

Also meaning "path" in Arabic, *shari'ah* guides all aspects of Muslim life, including daily routines, familial and religious obligations, and financial dealings. It is derived primarily from the Qur'an and the *sunnah*—the sayings, practices, and teachings of the Prophet Muhamad. Precedents and analogies applied by Muslim scholars help address new issues. The consensus of the Muslim community also plays a role in defining this theological manual.

In the eleventh century, to consolidate their control, the Sunni *ulama* crystallized their legal judgments into various schools of Islamic jurisprudence: the Sunni schools, Hanbali, Maliki, Ash-Shafe'i'i, Hanafi;

and the Shiite school, Ja'fari. Named after the scholars that inspired them, they differ in the weight each applies to the sources on which *shari'a* has its roots: the Qur'an, *hadith*, Islamic scholars, and community consensus.

Abu Hanifa (chronologically the first, 700–767), Malik ibn Anas (710–795), Muhammad ash-Ash-Shafe'i (767–820) and Ahmed ibn Hanbal (780–855) are the four Imams on whose work rests the foundations of Islamic jurisprudence and law. Although Hanifa's is the earliest, most tolerant and largest school—almost half of the Sunnis follow it—Ash-Shafe'i created the discipline of usul al-fiqh: (principles of jurisprudence, which laid the foundations for the first 'school' influencing the others.)

Several basic concepts in Islamic legal theory lay the foundation for a solution to modern-day perplexities. There is a distinction between *shari'ah*, the revealed way, and *fiqh*, the science of Islamic jurisprudence. In Islamic theology, *shari'ah* (lit. the way, the path to a water source) is the total of religious values and principles revealed to the Prophet Muhammad to direct human life. *Fiqh* (lit. understanding) is how humans derive concrete legal rules from the two primary sources of Islamic thought and practice: the Qur'an and the *sunnah* of the Prophet. As a concept, *shari'ah* cannot become a set of laws—it is closer to ethics than law. It embodies ethical values and principles that guide humans toward justice and correct conduct. What many commonly assert to be *shari'ah* laws, and therefore divine, are, in fact, often the result of *fiqh*, juristic activity, hence human, fallible and changeable.

There are two main categories of legal rulings: *'ibadat* (devotional/ spiritual acts) and *mu'amalat* (transactional/contractual acts). Rulings in the *'ibadat* category regulate relations between God and the believer, offering limited scope for change. Rulings in the *mu'amalat* category, however, regulate relations between humans and, therefore, remain open to change. Since human affairs constantly evolve, there is always a need for new rulings that use new interpretations of the religious texts to bring outdated laws in line with the changing realities of time and place (this is a concept recognised in Islamic jurisprudence known as *zaman wa makan*). It is the rationale for *ijtehad* (lit. endeavour, self-exertion), a method in Muslim jurisprudence for finding solutions to new issues in light of the guidance of revelation. Rulings concerning family and gender relations belong to the realm of *mu'amalat*, meaning that Muslim jurists have always considered them social and contractual matters open to rational consideration and change.

Diversity of opinion (*ikhtilaf*) is a fundamental concept that has always been a part of *fiqh*, even after the formal establishment of law schools. There is not now, nor has there ever been a single, unitary 'Islamic law'. There are multiple schools of Islamic law, and family laws in different countries vary widely, with individual provisions on every aspect of family life that differ considerably from country to country.

The very existence of multiple schools of law, along with the wide variety in Muslim family law provisions, attests to the fact that no one person, group or country can claim there is a unified, monolithic, divine Islamic law over which they have ownership. Within the context of the modern state, we must recognise and engage with this diversity of opinions to determine how best to serve the public interest (*maslahah*) and meet the demands of equality and justice.

Justice is inherent to the philosophy of law in Islam. Thus, statutes or legal amendments introduced in the name of *shari'ah* and Islam should reflect the values of equality, justice, love, compassion and mutual respect among all human beings. These are values and principles on which Muslims agree and which Muslim jurists hold to be among the indisputable objectives of the *shari'ah*, and are also consistent with universal human rights principles and values. In addition, historical events support the idea of equality between men and women regarding economic circumstances in marriage and family relations. The Qur'an introduced numerous reforms to existing cultural practices relating to financial provisions for women, including guaranteeing women's right to own, inherit, and dispose of property.

Reformation of Islam

The constant pressures from within to renew, change, and reform across the Muslim world are neither modern nor new; they represent the quest for the ideal in an imperfect world. Islam was constantly reviving after declining, always being re-discovered after being neglected. This revivalism or resurgence is not a twentieth-century phenomenon. The sense of déjà-vu, which permeates Muslim society, is not so much a reliving thing as recreating the past. The more the times change, the more certain societal features remain.

It would not be out of place to remember that great intellectual, Martin LingsHe feels that we have heard many times the words "development". (*tatawwur*) and "progress" (*taqaddum*) and "renewal" (*tajdîd*) and "renaissance" (*nahdah*), and perhaps it will not be a waste of time to pause and consider what they mean. "Development" means moving away from the principles. Although it is necessary to move a certain distance from the principles to make applications of them, it is vital to remain near enough for contact with them to be fully effective. Development must, therefore, never go beyond a certain point. Our ancestors knew this danger point had reached Islam hundreds of years ago. For us, who are so much further removed in time than we were from the ideal community of the Prophet and his companions, the danger is all the more significant. How, then, shall we presume not to be on our guard? How shall we not live in fear of increasing our distance from the principles to the point where development becomes degeneration? Indeed, most of what is valid today as development is not, in fact, degeneration. As for "progress, every individual should hope to progress, which is the meaning of our prayer: Guide us upon the way of transcendence.

The word "development" could also be used by individuals in the same positive sense. However, communities do not progress; if they did, what community was better qualified to progress than the first Islamic community in all the impetus of its youth? Yet the Prophet said, "The best of my people are my generation, then they that come after them, then they that come after those." We must conclude from the Qur'an that with the passage of the centuries, a general hardening of hearts is inevitable, for it says of one community, an extended length of time passed over them so that their hearts had hardened (QQ57: 16). The hope of communities must lie not in "progress" or "development" but in "renewal," that is, restoration. In its traditional, apostolic sense, renewal is the opposite of development, for it means a restoration of something of the primordial vigour of Islam. Renewal is, thus, a movement of return for Muslims, that is, a movement in a backwards rather than a forward direction.

There are and always have been multiple understandings and interpretations of Islamic law. *Ikhtilaf*, which means disagreement, difference of opinion and diversity of views, especially among the experts of Islamic law, is widely recognized and respected in the Islamic tradition. A fundamental principle of such jurisprudence is that each jurist can go back to the texts, examine the knowledge that has evolved, consider the new experiences and problems that arise, and develop new rulings based on the sound application of juristic methods. However, *fiqh* rulings on the family became literal expressions of the classical jurists' understanding of Islam's revealed text and their notions of justice, gender relations, and legal theories, reflecting their age's social and political realities. In that world, patriarchy and slavery were part of the fabric of society, seen as the natural order of things and a way to regulate social relations.

The quest for spiritual meaning is typically a personal matter in the West. In the Islamic world, it often leads the seeker into collective action, informed by utopian aspiration that admits no distinction between proselytizing, social reform, and politics. Renewal and reform—*in Arabic,* tajdid and islah—have an ambiguous and contested meaning in the Islamic world. They signify a stripping away of accumulated misreadings and wrong or lapsed practices, as in the Protestant Reformation, and a return to the founding texts of the Qur'an and the sunnah. But, beyond that, what is the nature of the reform? The traditional Sunni *ulama,* who had been subordinate to state power for centuries, had seen their role as guardians of the religious law restricted to family law and personal status.

The modernists distinguish the pristine faith and way of life of the Prophet and his first community from later manifestations, which resulted from the internationalization of Islam, its expansion outside of Arabia's borders, and a host of ultimately damaging acculturation processes. To derive the living value system as in its practical form was necessary; to justify its sacred origins, modernists require *ijtehad,* individual interpretation of scripture-and also the need for legal reform (perceived as separation of the true *shar'ia* from its medieval juridic formulation, the *fiqh*).

The modern thought in Islam

The Egyptian theocrat and jurist Muhammad Abduh argued that Islamic modernism's most crucial early representative in the Arab world combined professional expertise in Islamic theology and law with an awareness of Western modernity and scientific theories. To Abduh, Islam was eminently compatible with modernization. His main goal was to "renew" Muslim morality and reform the traditional social structures of his day, particularly his region, Egypt, by returning to the pristine and dynamic faith and morality of Islam's first generations. Reformation of Muslim society in that moral mould would bring about

Islamic modernism, indigenous and righteous, internally dynamic and externally powerful. Abduh approaches the Qur'anic text in new ways. He pays attention to the time and place of the revelations ("occasions of revelation"), emphasizes the literal meaning of the Qur'anic verses and their context, and largely de-emphasizes the *hadith*. By way of an interpretation "purified of foreign lore," Abduh seeks to rediscover the original meaning of the Qur'an, which shaped the faith and ethics of the "righteous forefathers" *(al-salafal-salih)*, that is the members of the first Muslim community, to recapture a sense of their morality for infusion into his society. Here, Abduh places great importance on the notions of woman's full humanity and equality with man before God, both because they are Qur'anic in origin and also because they are, in his opinion, indispensable in shaping a truly moral society.

The task of bringing Islamic precepts into line with modern realities resulted from the efforts of thinkers and leaders outside the' ulama ranks. Intellectuals and activists like the Indo-Pakistani Sayyid Abu'l Ala Mawdudi (d. 1979) and the Egyptian Sayyid Qutb were scholars without official ranking in the religious hierarchy. The radical movements they espoused (the Jamaat-i-Islami in South Asia and the Muslim Brotherhood in Egypt) contained modernist and traditional elements. A great contemporary in the field is the excellent philosopher-poet Mohammad Iqbal. To Iqbal, the Hellenic–Persian mysticism was 'nihilism'. He was bitter in his attacks against it. As he observed: "Having lost the vitality to grapple with the temporal, these prophets of decay apply themselves to the quest of a supposed eternal, and gradually complete the spiritual impoverishment and physical degeneration of their society by evolving a seemingly charming ideal of life which reduces the healthy and powerful to death". Iqbal refused to uphold the *status quo* in Islam; he attacked the closure of the doors of *ijtehad* and demanded the readjustment of Islamic principles to the needs of the present times.

Modern thought in Islam

Indeed, Iqbal is essentially a poet of Islam. Still, his Islam is not the Islam of primitive punishments, the veil and bigoted mullahs, but the Islam which provided a new light of thought and learning to the world and of heroic action and glorious deeds. He was devoted to the Prophet and believed in his message. Iqbal regarded the search for 'nullification' as the search for 'inner meanings' or 'hidden meanings' in either Muhammad's code or his way of life, which was found satisfying and convincing. He blamed the Persian poets for confusing the message of Islam. As he put it, "The Persian poets tried to undermine the way of Islam by a very roundabout, though apparently heart–alluring, manner. They denounced every good thing of Islam and made contemplation in a monastery the highest crusade in the way of God".

Iqbal, on the other hand, preached action. He was a rebel against all the accretions that had gathered around Islam as a result of the Hellenic and Persian influences and wanted to cleanse it so that the world could, once again, witness the glory of Islam in its pristine form. For the sloth and lethargy that had gripped the Islamic fold, Iqbal blamed the Sufis, who, with their Iranian background and Greek ideas, had corrupted the religion of Muhammad. As Iqbal explains, "It is surprising that the literature is a product of the period of political decline. The nation which exhausts its fund of energy and power, as was the case with the Muslims after the Tartar invasions, changes its outlook. The weakness becomes an object of beauty and appreciation, and resignation from the world is a source of satisfaction".

Iqbal's poems are a reflection of the pain and agony which he felt at the degeneration of Islam. This feeling is patent in every couplet. Iqbal repeatedly goaded Muslims to embrace the early era of Islam when the spirit of Muhammad guided his followers to conquer half the world and brought enlightenment to people of various regions and colours. While he admired the otherworldliness of Sufi mystics, he rejected their belief in the world's transitoriness and the unreality of life. While he was appalled by Western commercialism and greed, he lamented the loss of the Muslim empire and was disillusioned d by the decadence of Islam.

Dr Ali Shariaati, himself a legendary ideologue, writes, "If one were to reconstruct the form of Islam which has degenerated in the course of history, re-assemble it in such a way that the spirit could return to a total body, transform the present dazed elements into that spirit as if the trumpet of Israfil were to blow in the 20th century over a dead society and awaken its movement, power, spirit, and meaning, it is, then, that exemplary Muslim personalities will be reconstructed and reborn like Muhammad Iqbal."

The Iranian philosopher's visionary reinterpretation of Islam, resistance against Western influence and his role in inspiring the Iranian revolutionImperialistic thoughts and ideas were promulgated and adopted by the people, blunting their revolutionary instincts to the degree of obeisance. They were intoxicated with the ideas declaring Islam irrelevant and foggy to the modern challenges and demands. People had all lost their cultural and religious vigour. West-constructed values and ideas replaced Islamic values and principles.

The westernized Iranian generation abandoned religion, considering it useless to resolve their contemporary problems. It lacked utility for them. Ali Shariati decided to reinterpret the tenets of faith for them, explaining its relevance and resolution to modern Western ideologies. He opposed the prevailing interpretations of Islam and criticized the pseudo-scholars and clergies of his time. Marxist and secular critics consider him anti-ulema and anti-Islamic state. It is a fabrication. He wanted ulemas to be responsible and intellectuals to understand the layered misinterpretation of Islam and its beliefs. He divided Shiism into two into two thoughts: Alawi and Safavid Shiism. The former is radical, revolutionary, active and committed to social justice, whereas the latter is conservative and politically quiescent.

Like Allama Iqbal and Shaheed Mutahhari, he undertook the mission of liberating Islam from the hegemonic clutches of the West. He stressed adopting the proper methods of understanding Islam and its valid message and practising it through one's conduct. He was not against ulemas, but he wanted them to know how colonizing and atheistic ideology works secretly to undermine the fundamental and pristine message of Islam. He decoded the true meaning of tawhid (monotheism). He interprets it as a resistance to despotic rulers and a struggle for a better society where justice, equality and peace remain the main emblems.

Ali Shariati learned from Frantz Fanon that our understanding of religion, culture, and civilization can become more profound, vastly deeper, and broader if we return to Islam's original roots and grasp critical ideals. Ali Shariati studied religion historically to tease out distortions. He was a sociologist who went through religion's social and historical dimensions. He says that to know someone or something, we should adopt two approaches to study it. First, we should know about a person's books, articles, and speeches. Secondly, we should see the history and society of someone or something. He treated Islam as a human being and analyzed it through its history and the society in which it was practised and implemented.

One can learn about Islam through the Qur'an and the thoughts and ideas of great Islamic thinkers, scholars, and chroniclers of hadith. He believes Islam is a religion whose objective is to make a better society. He critiques the scholars, clergies and philosophers who ignored social realities. He praises Aviccena for his intellect but criticizes him for being ignorant of many important aspects of society. The purpose of religion is to develop the social life of a human being in addition to his individual life. Shariati reinterpreted the Quran to awaken people to their social and historical role. Similarly, he addressed the theological doctrines by adopting a unique approach.

The foundations of our ancestors

The lives of our great ancestors can be a catalyst for rethinking 'Muslim womanhood' as a socially and historically constructed identity. It is essential for women living in Muslim societies to know and understand their history for themselves and popularize it among their sisters. Their lives are elucidatory examples of women who defied culturally defined gender norms to assert their right to be different and to change their society. We must understand the importance of historical narratives and not treat them as a mere collection of stories. By telling us who we have been, history defines a sense of self that funnels into and guides a sense of potential tomorrow for a person.

The majority of ordinary Muslim women remain mired in local, tribal codes and customs that do not permit them to benefit from their Islamic heritage. Islam itself remains only half understood. The recovery from the colonial past has been too slow and painful, and the sense of the future is uncertain. Until Muslim scholars and intellectuals can come to terms with history, they cannot repair the damage. The success of a few outstanding women will do little to improve the unsatisfactory lot of the majority of Muslim women. Only with widespread education and the restoration of Muslim confidence can contemporary Muslim women assume their rightful place in society: it is only then that the Prophet's saying about paradise lying at the feet of the mother will have meaning.

Liberation of women from oppression

One of the reasons for the establishment of Islam was to liberate women. It gave them equal civil status with men through the right to own property, inherit, divorce petition, and receive an education, amongst many other entitlements. The Prophet's wife, Khadija, was a prominent businesswoman and the first person to accept Islam whilst reassuring her husband of his Prophethood. It was not until post-Muhammad, with the codification of the laws and the development of Islamic jurisprudence, that women's role in society became limited. It can be due to the motivation of some men to interpret the Qur'an and hadith literature to reflect the cultural nuances of the time.

While it is necessary to keep reminding ourselves about the incredible transformation that Islam has wrought in the nascent Muslim community, it is equally important that we take lessons from them. The past must redeem the future. It is a plain wistfulness to rest on the laurels of the legacy left behind by our illustrious forbears and keep drumming about the golden age without being inspired by the glorious trail blazed by the early Muslim women. Let us remember the advice of the great poet Percy Bysshe Shelley:

> The world's great age begins anew,
> The golden years return,
> The earth doth like a snake renew.
> Her winter weeds were outworn;
> Heaven smiles, and faiths and empires gleam
> Like wrecks of a dissolving dream. [...]
> The world is weary of the past—
> O might it die or rest at last!

(Hellas: Chorus)

Iqbal has portrayed these sentiments very poignantly in his poem *Complaint and Answer*. In the first poem, the poet complains to God about the downfall of the Muslim c; community and their continuing and humiliating defeats at the hands of the infidels. The second poem is an imagined reply of God to the "complaint" of the poet. Here is one verse from the lament of Muslims:

> *Once in the fray, a firm we stood our ground, never did we yield,*
> *The most lion-hearted of our foes reeled back and fled the field.*
> *Those who rose against You, against them we turn our ire,*
> *What cared we for their sabers? We fought against canon fire.*

On every human heart the image of Your Oneness we drew,
Beneath the daggers point, we proclaimed your message true

In response to Muslims' plaint of sorrow at having been let down by God, they receive an answer:

You have no strength in your hands; in your hearts, God has no place;
On the name of my messenger, you people have brought disgrace.
Destroyers of false gods are gone; only the idol maker thrives;
There were days when every Muslim loved the only Allah he knew;
Once upon a time, He was your only Beloved; the same Beloved you
now call untrue.
Who blotted out the smears of falsehood from the pages of history?
Who freed mankind from the chains of slavery?
The floors of my Kaaba with whose foreheads swept?
Who were they who clasped my Qur'an to their breasts?
Your forefathers indeed were; tell us who you are, we pray.
With idle hands, you sit, awaiting the dawn of a better day.

In Islam, renewal and revolution continue to give it dynamism and life. Islamic fervour knows no national boundaries, no class differences, no racial barriers. Throughout history, it has transcended these. Islam emphasizes belief and behaviour over race and practice, not blood. It is essential to how people behave, their customs, culture, and society are structured, and not who their ancestors were. Islam, in the ideal, believes in 'nurture', not 'nature'; it transcends class and nation. Fazlur Rahman writes in his book Islam and Modernity: "A historical critique of theological developments in Islam is the first step toward reconstructing Islamic theology. This critique should reveal the extent of the dislocation between the world view of the Qur'an and various schools of theological speculation in Islam and point the way toward a new theology." If Muslims had seriously understood this philosophy, they would have benefited the Islamic world immensely. For him, it was the intellectual ossification and replacement of scholarship based on original thought by one based on commentaries and super-commentaries, the closing of the gate of *ijtehad*, and the basing of the Islamic method solely on taqlid (blind imitation and the following of predecessors)) which led to the decline.

Fazlur Rahman's revolutionary thought

Fazlur Rahman's goal was to reassess the Islamic intellectual tradition and provide a way forward for Muslims. In his view, re-examining Islamic methodology in the light of the Qur'an itself was a prerequisite for any reform in Islamic thought. Rahman incredibly stressed the ethical aspect of the Qur'an. The traditional theology concerned itself more with ritualistic aspects than ethical, though it did not entirely neglect it.

Rahman says: "Muslim scholars have never attempted an ethics of the Qur'an, systematically or otherwise. Yet, no one who has carefully studied the Qur'an can fail to be impressed by its ethical fervour. Indeed, ethics is its essence and the necessary link between theology and law. The Qur'an tends to concretise the ethical, clothe the general in a particular paradigm, and translate the ethical into legal or quasi-legal commands. But it is precisely the sign of its moral vigour that it is not content only with generalisable ethical propositions but is keen on translating them into actual paradigms. However, the Qur'an always explains the objectives or principles that are the essence of its laws."

Rahman firmly believed that one of the primary purposes of the Qur'ān was to create a society based on justice. He saw the Prophet Muḥammad as a social reformist who sought to empower the impoverished, the weak, and the vulnerable. The Prophet regarded the Qur'ān as a source from which ethical principles could emanate, and it was not just a book of laws. The Prophet played the roles of father, husband, chief, warrior, friend, and Prophet. His respect for learning, tolerance of others, generosity of spirit, concern for the weak, gentle piety and desire for a better, cleaner world would constitute the main elements of the Muslim ideal. For Muslims, the life of the Prophet is the triumph of hope over despair, light over darkness. For instance, Rahman argues that the family law in Islamic history did not accord females the equal rights to which they were entitled, following the Prophet's example and the teachings of the Qur'ān.

Rahman's primary contribution to the debate on the Qur'ān in the twentieth century was that he emphasised that if we wanted to get authentic insights into the Qur'ān, Muslims needed to move away from reductionist and formulaic approaches to the Qur'ān, which were incapable of recognising its social, historical, and linguistic context. His emphasis on the context of revelation has far-reaching influenced contemporary Muslim debates on critical issues such as human rights, women's rights, and social justice. Rahman argued that without being aware of the social and political conditions of the society in which the Qur'ān appeared, one could not fully understand its message. Thus, the emphasis is on the "context."

Arkoun's interpretation

The well-known Islamic scholar from the West, Mohammad Arkoun, is highly critical of the past and present conditions of Islamic thought and contemporary Islamic societies. He says that its spiritual transformative power over the hearts and minds of Muslims had eroded. In his view, the spiritual essence of the covenant between God and man has been allowed to deteriorate into legal codes, rituals and ideologies of domination in the interest of religious and political elites. He argues that the outstanding cultural achievements of the early Islamic era in bringing together Qur'anic revelation and Greek rational philosophic humanism have long been closed.

Arkoun believes the Qur'an must be experienced anew as a religious revelation that brings about an inner transformation and inspires a trust and holy love of God that transcends all ritual, legal, communal and institutional forms. This renewal of revelation depends on a revival of the intellectual, scientific, humanistic Islamic culture of the classical era (a Muslim renaissance that would allow for thinking of the hitherto unthought in Islam) and the assimilation of the industrial and information revolutions, with their modern social, scientific, theological and philosophical insights.

The exordiums in the following verses of the Qur'an are very enlightening:

- Believers, take warning, then, O ye with eyes (to see) (Q59:2)

- We have sent down to thee the Book in truth, that thou mightest judge between men, as guided by Allah. So, be not (used) as an advocate by those who betray their trust (Q4:105).

- Behold, in this also is a sign for those who are wise. (Q16:67)

- We did indeed offer the Trust to the Heavens and the Earth and the Mountains; but they refused to undertake it, being afraid thereof: but man undertook it;- He was indeed unjust and foolish (Q33-72)

- For had it not been for Allah's repelling some men by means of others, cloisters and churches and oratories and mosques, wherein the name of Allah is oft mentioned, would assuredly have been pulled down (Q 22:40)

- And hold fast, all together, by the rope which Allah (stretches out for you), and be not divided among yourselves; and remember with gratitude Allahs favour on you; for ye were enemies, and He joined your hearts in love, so that by His Grace, ye became brethren; and ye were on the brink of the pit of Fire, and He saved you from it. Thus doth Allah make His Signs clear to you: That ye may be guided. (Q3:103)

The concepts of gender equality and human rights—as we mean them today—had no place and little relevance to the classical jurists' conceptions of justice. They were, in Arkoun's terms, 'unthinkable' for premodern Muslim jurists and thus remained 'unthought' in Islamic legal thought. The ideas of human rights and gender equality belong to the modern world. As the pre-modern notions of marriage in Islamic legal theory lose their theological validity and their power to convince, the discourses of feminism and human rights have combined to bring a new consciousness and a new point of reference for Muslim women and reformist thinkers. The ideas of equal rights for women and equality in the family are among the ones that use the *fiqh* idiom, the 'newly created issues' (*masa'il mustahdatha*) that pose a challenge to Islamic legal thought.

Modern Islamic jurisprudence

Modern scholars of Islamic jurisprudence are reviving the traditional tools and methodologies to re-read and understand Islamic sources and use classical juristic principles such as *ikhtilaf* (diversity within Islamic law and *fiqh*), *istihsan* (adopting the idea or principle that is better, more useful), *maslahah* (choosing that which benefits the public interest or common good), *ijtehad*(exerting effort to form an independent judgment on a legal question), and *maqasid al-shari'ah* (the objectives of the *shari'ah*) to develop solutions for the 'newly created issues'. Working with progressive scholars to better understand these tools and their possibilities is one way to open the dialogue about equality in Muslim laws and practices instead of simply stating that change is impossible. If 'Islam is the solution', if Islam is relevant for all times, and if Islam is supposed to bring justice, then it is legitimate and imperative for governments to engage with scholars to search for new solutions to the conflicts and tensions that arise as a result of the disconnect between women's lived realities and Islamic law as traditionally defined. The trajectory for reform and the possibilities for equality and justice exist within Islamic legal thought. But this effort towards a more just society through a more just understanding of Islam must be an inclusive effort that represents the needs and interests, in particular, of those who suffer the injustices and effects of discrimination. Leaving it as the exclusive preserve of the traditionalists in religious authority has only sustained unjust patriarchal understandings of Islam.

Some scholars, however, have continued to search for Islamic answers to the questions of modern life. Contrary to the claims of secularists who deny the compatibility of Islam and contemporary notions of women's rights, Islamic attitudes on the question vary pretty widely. According to "Islamic feminists," Islam is actually a very progressive religion for women, was radically egalitarian for its time, and remains so in some of its scriptures. They contend that Islamic law has evolved in ways that are inimical to gender equality, not because it pointed in that direction but because of selective interpretation by patriarchal leaders and a mingling of Islamic teachings with tribal customs and traditions. Islamic feminists now seek to revive the equality bestowed on women in the religion's early years by rereading the Qur'an, putting the Scriptures in context, and disentangling them from tribal practices. One of the significant milestones in political Islam's revolutionary history was the Arab Spring. It also had several implications for theocratic Islam.

What did the Arab Spring accomplish?

"Arab Spring" was first used by American conservative commentators but has since been challenged as an inadequate misnomer. Since 2011, the goals of many Arab Spring protesters have been an autocratic government to regain power and crack down on civil liberties. Nonetheless, the uprisings have shown the power of mass demonstrations and peaceful protest, as well as social media's ability to fuel protest and communicate its goals to the outside world. The tumult of the Arab Spring also showed autocratic governments—and the rest of the world—that millions of people living in Islamic nations believe in free expression and democratic governance. The debate about the relationship between Islam and democracy conclusively ended with the coming of the Arab Spring.

Islam is at a crossroads today, and Muslims are at a critical juncture in their history. The stagnation in Islamic thought is patent in the couplets of Iqbal:

You are one people; you share in common your weal and woe
You have one faith, one creed and to one Prophet allegiance owe
You have one sacred Ka'aba, one God and one holy book, the Qur'an
Was it so difficult to unite every single Mussalman in one community?
It is factions in one place and divisions into castes in another
In these times are these the ways to progress and prosper?

⸺⸻◦⸻⸺

You are bent on self destruction; for honour and self respect they were known.
Brotherly feelings are alien to you; for brothers' lives they gave their own
All you do is talk and talk; they were men of action, deeds and power;
You hanker after little buds; theirs was the garden and every flower
To this day the peoples of the world remember tales of their glory
Their righteous deeds are written on the scrolls of history

It is time we dissolve our mutual acrimonies and apply our intellect and energies tao the pursuit of realizing the Qur'anic vision.

A Muslim has free will and the power to rebel and surrender. Thus, he or she is responsible and the maker of his or her own image. "Every soul is held in pledge for what he earns." (Q74:38) "And the human being shall have nothing but what he strives for." (Q53:30) We need to be earnest in our efforts to let the path be enlightened.

You attain to knowledge by argument;
You attain a craft or skill by practice;
If voluntary poverty's your choice,

companionship's the way, not hand or tongue.
The knowledge of it passes soul to soul,
not by way of talk or reams of notes.
Its signs are writ upon the seeker's heart,
yet still, the seeker cannot keep those signs
until his heart becomes exposed to light
Then God reveals His: Did We not expose? [Qur'an 94:1]
For We've exposed the chambers of your breast
and placed the exposition in your heart

(Rumi, *Masnavi* 5: 1062-7)

Muslims need to adopt a revolutionary approach

To be faithful to their scientific heritage, Muslims need to do much more than preserve the ashes of its fire; they need to transmit its flame.

The great philosopher-poet Sir Muhammad Iqbal summed up the Muslim dilemma very pithily:

alfaz-o-maani mein tafawat nahin lekin
mullah ki azan aur, mujahid ki azan aur
parwaz hai dono ki issi aik faza mein
kargas ka jahan aur hai, shaheen ka jahan aur

(There is no speck of difference between words and meanings.
But the clarion call of a prayer caller and guerilla are poles apart.
the vulture and falcon soar in the same skies
But the world of falcons and vultures is far different)

For Muslims, therefore, it is an excellent time to pause, to reflect, and to attempt to re-locate the main features of, to re-discover, Islam. God says in the Qur'ān that a people's condition will not change until they change in themselves (Q13:11). We, therefore, take stock, not because we have arrived at any significant stage of the Islamic journey but because of the sheer range of trajectories and approaches and consequent confusion, obliges us to attempt clarification. The problem is not that there are too few answers but too many. To put it in the words of the Qur'an: "Those who listen to the Word and follow the best (meaning) in it: those whom Allah has guided and those endowed with understanding." (Q39:18)

Roots of rage

Islam was a vast empire stretching from western Africa into India. An empire that valued learning, prized scholars, maintained great libraries and preserved the works of many ancient writers. But within three centuries, this greatest civilisation on the face of the earth was in retreat, and the West was rising to produce a civilisation renowned for its commitment to personal liberty, scientific expertise, political democracy, and free markets.

By the time of the death of the Prophet Mohammed in 632, most of the tribes of the Arabian Peninsula had united under the banner of Islam, some out of faith, others from expediency. But few people outside Arabia knew who Muslims were or were worried about the threat they might pose. The world of Islam was once the foremost military and economic power of its kind and the leader in the arts and sciences of civilisation. Christian Europe was labelled to be brutal and remote. Then, there was a sudden do; downfall. It was downhill from then on, and this is where the Muslim world finds itself. Muslims centred their identity upon the duality of religion and politics embodied in the ummah (community of believers) until the twilight of the last Islamic caliphate, the Ottoman Empire (1290-1924).

The ummah prided itself on the vastness and the holistic aspect of Islam and its human achievements. It was timeless, representing Muslims' past and future and spatially leaving no boundaries, stretching the entire known world. It was neither a government nor a theocracy but a congregation of faith. From the Crusades of the eleventh century to the Turkish expansion of the fifteenth century to the colonial era in the early twentieth century, Islam and the West have often battled militarily. This tension has existed for hundreds of years, during which many periods of peace and even harmony exist. Until the 1950s, for example, Jews and Christians lived peaceably under Muslim rule. Bernard Lewis, the pre-eminent historian of Islam, has argued that for much of history, religious minorities did better under Muslim rulers than they did under Christian ones.

Islam is compatible with modern technology

Muslim scholars insist that nothing in Islam is incompatible with technological advances or industrial development. In the days of the caliphs, Islam led the world in scientific and intellectual discoveries. What Muslims object to are the evils associated with modernisation. The breakdown of the family structure, the lowering of moral standards, and the appeal of easygoing secular lifestyles. At the same time, Muslims are demanding the positive best of the West, such as schools, hospitals, income avenues and technology.

For a time, the secret of Western success seemed to lie in two achievements: economic advancement, especially in industry, and political evolution. Several generations of reformers and modernisers tried to adapt these ideas and introduce them to their own countries in the hope that they would thereby be able to achieve equality with the West and restore their lost superiority. In our own time, this mood of admiration and emulation has, among many Muslims, given way to one of hostility and rejection. This mood partly resulted from a feeling of humiliation and growing awareness among the heirs of an old, proud, and long-dominant civilisation which had been overborne and overwhelmed by those they looked upon as their inferiors.

Introspection among Muslims

Muslims are now taking a keen interest in understanding the truth and reality to creatively use it to adopt modern ways without losing the religious principles underpinning their faith. There are two schools of thought among Muslims: one that believes that religion must concede space to embrace modernization, and the other that wants modernization must also allow space for the sake of religion. Between them, there is now a third, whose number is growing; it sees a possibility of reconciling the modern impulses of life with the traditional ethos of religion. It finds in the principles an ample space of liberalism that provides people with scope for leading modern life without compromising faith. A Muslim has free will and is the maker of their image. "every soul has to pledge for what he earns." (q74:38) "and the human being shall have nothing but what he strives for." (Q 53:30)

Islam is now going through a significant shift unlike any other it has experienced. There have been muted and vocal rumblings, stressing a need for reform and reinterpretation to make Islam relevant to the modern context. There have also been consistent attempts to make the clerics recognise the non-clerical perspective in formulating an Islamic response to the present times and its complexities and vicissitudes. It is now universally acknowledged that liberal and progressive interpretations that can answer our doubts and confusions need a more profound and nuanced reading of the Qur'an and *sunnah*. It calls for a more varied understanding so that the Qur'an becomes accessible for examination in the light of modern knowledge and wisdom. Conservatism has been an ally for all these ages, but Muslims can no longer afford to delay their response to the new challenges and dilemmas that had perplexed the minds of many of our predecessors.

Muslims must not lose sight of certain fundamental beliefs in their quest for theological interpretation. Islam (and religion) is about being a good human being. It involves showing empathy, compassion and charity to others. Seeking strength and comfort through prayer and communal bonhomie is vital, as is reaching out to the unknown and seeking guidance and mercy in the world. That is what Islam is for the ordinary man, and that is what is needed to rescue it from the literalists.

Muslims are now responsive to change and attempting to develop a more modern and humane interpretation of Islam, and some countries are undergoing significant transformations. More and more Muslims now perceive those erroneous interpretations ofIslamic law that are highly unjust to women and appear to have become obsolete.

For Muslims, it is an excellent time to pause, reflect, and attempt to re-locate the main features of and re-discover Islam. Muslims should, therefore, take stock not just because they have been at a critical intersection of the Islamic journey but because the sheer range of trajectories and approaches and accompanying confusion obliges them to attempt an appraisal. The issue is not that there are too few answers but too many. To put it in the words of the Qur'an: "Those who listen to the word and follow the best (meaning) in it: those are the ones whom Allah has guided, and those are the ones endued with understanding". (Q39:18)

* * * * *

5. TABLIGHI JAMAAT: A CARAVAN OF MISUNDERSTOOD MISSIONARIES

Let there arise out of you a band of people inviting to all that is good, enjoining what is right, and forbidding what is wrong: They are the ones to attain felicity.

– (Qur'an 3: 104)

In recent years, clichéd calls for reform of Islam have intensified. "we need a Muslim reformation," "Islam needs reformation from within", and "an urgent need for a reappraisal of Islam" scream in the usual headlines through newspapers and airwaves. Reforms across the crisis-ridden Muslim-majority world may not be highly essential: political, socio-economic and, yes, religious too. But more important and urgently relevant and meaningful is that Muslims need to rediscover their heritage of pluralism, tolerance and mutual respect – embodied in, say, the prophet's letter to the monks of St Catherine's monastery, or the "convivencia" (or co-existence) of medieval Muslim Spain.

Concept of da'wah

Da'wah is among the primary drivers of Islamic expansion. It is one of the leading ways to convert non-Muslims. Islamic da'wah implies outreach to a person who is not a Muslim and inviting them to accept the faith of Islam. Islam, being a missionary religion, requires Muslims to teach their beliefs to others to persuade and convince them to convert. Each Muslim has to share the beliefs of Islam with a non-Muslim and invite them to Islam.

Da'wah refers to the mission strategy the Muslims use to make people become Muslims. It is expected of Muslims that they do it quietly and respectfully. Muslims see da'wah as a vital tool in their search for world dominance. *Da'wah's* mission is distinct from the Christian and has led to conversion from Christianity to Islam.

As humans, we must acknowledge that we, regardless of the religion we are adherents of, should be free to hold our unique points of view and express our ideas without fear. No one has the privilege of claiming to know God more than others. Therefore, we must let individuals establish their relationship with God and understand Him in a relevant personal manner rather than an institutional one.

Da'wah is among the primary drivers of Islamic growth. It is one of the leading ways to convert non-Muslims. Islamic da'wah is best defined as outreach to a person who is not a Muslim and inviting them to accept the faith of Islam. Islam, being a missionary religion, requires Muslims to teach their beliefs to others to persuade and convince them to convert. Each Muslim shares the beliefs of Islam with a non-Muslim and invites them to Islam. Da'wah refers to the mission strategy the Muslims use to make people become Muslims. It is undertaken quietly and respectfully. Muslims see da'wah as a vital tool in their search for world dominance. Da'wah's mission has led to conversion from Christianity to Islam.

In these times of religious rift and growing religious conflict, we must promote religious inclusiveness, accept our differences and learn to coexist without imposing our religious notions of God on other individuals and communities. Religion must serve the purpose of making us more human and binding us to God and humanity at large without tainting our minds with ideas of superiority, exclusivity and intolerance.

For most Muslims, religion cannot be limited strictly to the realm of personal faith and private life: Islam has many things to say about society and what it stipulates as a just order. Unlike Christianity, Islam was concerned with politics and governance from the start: the Muslim rule that developed in the prophet's lifetime required attention to principles of community life, justice, administration, relations with non-muslims, defence and foreign policy. A vision of what constitutes good governance, law and a just society were among the principal new ideas ushered by Islam. The prophet came not to protect the status quo but to reform and change it. Women, for instance, were given legal status (where they had none before) and sound legal protection within society. Islam's scripture contains three times as many passages urging Muslims to think, rethink, and apply their minds judiciously instead of promoting and practising blind worship.

Islam needs vigorous rejuvenation

The Muslim world is admittedly in crisis, and a biased media has brushed its negative colour to exaggerate the conflicts that are plaguing the Islamic planet. This negative stereotyping creates an impression that everything Muslim is evil. However, away from this glare, a silent revolution is underway, with a mission that Prophet Muhammad placed at the top of his priorities – the spread of the authentic message of Islam. Called *da'wah* – the concept of propagation of Islamic faith-a massive army of preachers is silently transforming the lives of those who have no perception, or perhaps an erroneous perception, of Islam.

Religions have jostled with each other for millenniums. Many of today's missionaries are returning to practices of proselytizing abandoned long ago by the mainline missionaries. Armed only with sleeping bags, backpacks, and a simple message, *da'wah* activists go door-to-door in more than 200 countries. They are more active in Africa or the Caribbean, where evangelism and religious competition are jostling but allowing each other to thrive. They are easily recognised and are unfailingly polite. This mission evokes tales of Prophet Muhammad's companions who trekked hundreds of miles and braved bandits and armies to spread the word of Islam back in the 7th century.

Emerging challenges of modernism

Now, in the age of modern technology, the hardships are fewer, but challenges and prejudices are much more severe. But, if the Prophet's companions could sacrifice their lives to propagate Islam, present-day Muslims can emulate them in a much more significant way. *Da'wah* means the issuing of a summons, call or invitation. It is an essential duty of every Muslim to invite people to their faith or to recall nominal or lapsed Muslims to a deeper faith. A Muslim who practices *da'wah* as a preacher, religious worker or in faith-building community work is called a Da'i, plural Du'at.

Islam's propagation is a cardinal duty of every Muslim. It is particularly relevant in modern times, where negative stereotyping of Muslims has brought a bad name to the faith. It also underlines the importance of the participation of educated Muslims because the knowledge explosion requires more sophisticated intellectual equipment to navigate the complex religious landscape.

For Islamic civilization, a flawless moral character is a fundamental framework for a righteous human being. This trait distinguishes Islamic civilization from its counterparts. The argument that other civilizations, too, have a moral foundation is the fact that Islam is a way of life – ad-Deen – and not simply a religion. Our values shape our lives; they are the qualities that define us. They make us who we are, guide us in our life choices, and make us what we believe in and what we commit to. It is, finally, our conduct that will influence the perception of others about us. These markers are the assumptions around which Islam finds its soul.

Islam has a simple but highly effective evangelical message that mirrors Islam's five cardinal pillars of practice: grasp the true meaning and implications of the creedal statement that there is no deity except Allah, and Muhammad is his messenger; pray conscientiously five times a day; acquire learning and engage in the frequent remembrance of God; honour fellow believers; and participate in missionary work (*da'wah*) by spreading awareness of Islam. Da'wah is God's way of bringing believers to faith. Historically, missionary *da'wah* accompanied commercial ventures or followed military conquests. The "invitation", or call, to accept Islam has been extended not just to non-Muslims but also to Muslims who do not observe Islam in its entire form. Calling non-Muslims and "inconsistent" Muslims to Islam is considered by Muslim theologians to be an unconditional duty of every Muslim missionary of Islam.

The *da'wah* message is nonviolent and harbours no hatred for other faiths or peoples. Instead, it seeks to show Muslims that the injustice and oppression they face are symptoms of their waning morality. It insists that the solution lies in spiritual renewal. The aim is less about conversion and more about propagating their view of correct Qur'anic teachings about sin and salvation.

Da'wah supporters lay out two simple aims in their lessons drawn from Qur'anic verses and the recorded sayings of Prophet Muhammad. First, they encourage fellow Muslims to return to what they believe are the standards and morals of the prophet's companions. Second, they recruit, asking worshipers to join *da'wah* and participate in Kharooj. Kharooj is the designated mission defined by the number of days involved in the spiritual journey, typically three days, 40 days or four months. We can pursue *da'wah* through writing, speaking and personal conduct. The best *da'wah* is through demonstration of one's good conduct.

The most accomplished modern missionary is Muhammad Ilyas Kandhalvi (d. 1944). When he began his revivalist movement called Tablighi Jamaat (proselytizing group) in a rural setting in Mewat, India, in 1927, it responded to a dominant Hindu culture that Muslims feared could sweep away centuries of Islamic norms and traditions. Kandhalvi wanted to take his teachings from the classroom to ordinary people. The Meos, who were Muslims, mostly followed several Hindu traditions. The members of the group are popularly known as "Tablighis".

Over the past century, what began as a revivalist movement has transformed into a global phenomenon. It has seen a massive surge in recent times, heightened by an intense religious zeal in the new generation of Muslims. Although its members are from diverse backgrounds, all share one critical common interest—the propagation of Islam for the salvation of souls. The movement has an amazingly well-oiled machine that nets thousands of new followers yearly.

Tablighi Jamat's movement on the ground level

Every day, thousands of groups of *da'wah* followers go on Kharooj. Like Jehovah's Witnesses, they trawl through the day to save souls and find new converts for their faith. They approach people door-to-door, give a two-minute speech, bless the people they visit, and make one request: that they join them for prayer and a brief lecture at the neighbourhood mosque. Instead of adopting the frayed coarse discourses, the Da'is use exciting anecdotes from the Islamic scriptures to enthuse the initiates. With the enlightened elders, they also engage in deep theological discussions. The two essential books which serve as intellectual tools for these proselytizers are Fazail-e-Amaal (Virtues of Deeds) by Maulana Zakaria Kandhalvi and Muntakhaba Ahadith (Selected Sayings of Prophet Muhammad).

Tablighi Jamaat acts as a beacon to those lost in Jahiliyyah (the state of ignorance of guidance from God), but it stops short of that. *As Travellers in Faith* says, "Man is a ship in a tumultuous sea. It is impossible to repair it without removing it from the high seas where the waves of ignorance and the temptations of temporal life assail it. Its only chance is to come back to land to be dry-docked. The dry dock is the mosque of the Jamaat."

Many proselytizing groups have seen a theological trend in producing impactful outcomes, such as using education and healthcare as add-on activities as part of proselytisation. The Tablighis practice is purely preaching and propagating their faith knowledge. Transnationalism and travel are two distinct characteristics of this movement. It adopted transnational travel and physical movement as a means of *da'wah*. For God's sake, the most important and frequent activity of an adept of the Jamaat is going out. A combination of time and space, 'travel' has a special meaning in the Tablighi discourse. Tablighi Jamaat members leave the comfort of their homes for 3 to 4 months to serve God. During these self-financed treks. The members travel to different cities, villages, or towns, stay at a mosque there, and go door to door, reminding Muslims to study the Quran and pay more attention to Islam. Intoxicants are off-limits, but missionaries have to shun gossip and vain talks to concentrate their mind on the task at hand,

The Islamic evangelical movement is comparable to the concept of Hijrah, which witnesses a similar phenomenon of migration and withdrawal. It is travel within oneself, moulding our spiritual personality's contours. One temporarily migrates from *duniya* (worldly pursuits) to *deen* (religious concerns), a favourite dichotomy among the Tablighis. It is a migration from contamination to purity, drawing away from worldly attachments to the path of God. A spiritual period in a Tabligh is a retreat that reduces the temptation of earthly pleasures and defines the individuals' spiritual trajectory by setting them on the path to the world hereafter.

The philosophy of the Tabligh movement

An important point a Da'i must emphasize is that the Islamic concept of spirituality differs from that of other religions. In contrast to the renunciation of the world and physical self-denial, the Tabligh has a unique paradigm of being in the midst of life, facing all the difficulties and hardships, and performing all the activities with the sole objective of seeking the pleasure of God. He must understand that he is God's vicegerent and must fulfil this role's obligations.

Far from proselytizing and inducing others to change their religion or way of life against their free will, Islam does not permit the use of coercive, aggressive or violent efforts even while encouraging people for the common good of the whole of humankind. To set an example, *da'wah* followers attempt to emulate the social practices of Muhammad in all aspects of life, ranging from which foot should exit the mosque first to which direction to face when sleeping at night. They eat from communal platters on the ground, men sport beards of a certain length, and use Miswak (teeth-cleaning twig) instead of a toothbrush as did the Prophet's companions.

The Qur'an has made it explicitly clear that the Islamic call (da'wah) and preaching (*balagh*) method should be fair, balanced, moderate, peaceful and non-violent so that listeners are captivated by the pitch of the invitation. The Qur'anic term "balagh" means "to convey the message" and" not to convert". It is a product of the application of wisdom and prudence on the preacher's part.

Before they start on Qur'anic matters, the missionaries must connect with people personally. They should enquire with them about their families, lives, and adversities and respond to their issues with sensitivity. They must avoid being pedantic and try to coax them with affection. These two Qur'anic verses are highly relevant for the missionaries:

- "You cannot guide whoever you please: it is God who guides whom He will" (Q28:56)

- "It is not up to you to guide them, but Allah guides whom He wills." (Q2:72)

The proselytisation movement must guard itself against the arrogance that bedevilled such movements in the past. The missionaries must inculcate the highest ethical standards as enunciated in the Qur'an. They must creatively leverage the humanitarian or educational platform to share the "gospel."

In today's complex world, we need innovative missionaries trained in strategic thinking to devise multiple ways of communicating the "gospel" through cultural filters and societal barriers. The overarching objective of the missionary must finally be to see that all people in the population segment become evangelized and can ingrain a transparent faith in their psyche.

* * * * *

6. CAN SALAFIS AND SUFIS MEET ON A COMMON GROUND

In Islam, renewal and revolution continue to give it dynamism and life. The Islamic value system knows no class differences, national boundaries, or racial barriers. Throughout history, it has transcended them. It is essential to how people behave, their customs, culture, and society, not who their ancestors were. The idea that Islam believes in is in 'nurture', not 'nature'; it transcends class and nation.

There is a tendency on the part of some Muslim scholars to exaggerate the accomplishments of Islamic science. and they don't need to be exaggerated. During the golden age of Islamic science, which ended somewhere between. 1100 and 1200, Muslim scientists were way ahead of their contemporaries in Christian Europe. It emerges when people talk about the decline of Muslim science, which some scholars of Muslim civilization think was real. Others vociferously defend the continued excellence of Muslim science. When the scientific revolution came, it first benefited Europe, not the world of Islam. For example, Muslims kept building observatories, which aided them in making very accurate measurements of the apparent motions of the sun, moon, and stars.

However, even after European astronomers began using telescopes, none of the astronomers in the Muslim world used telescopes until modern times. That's because they weren't building those observatories to do science. They were building them to make religious calendars and determine the direction to Mecca. The great modern scholar Fazlur Rahman writes in his book *Islam and Modernity*: "A historical critique of theological developments in Islam is the first step toward a reconstruction of Islamic theology. This critique should reveal the extent of the dislocation between the world view of the Qur'an and various schools of theological speculation in Islam and point the way toward a new theology." For Rahman, it was the intellectual ossification and replacement of scholarship based on original thought by one based on commentaries and super-commentaries, the closing of the gate of *ijtehad* (and basing of Islamic method solely on taqlid (mindlessly following the views of past scholars) which led to the decline.

The erratic rhythm of modern life

There is a growing feeling of desolation and misery as we find the world trapped in chaos. The pace of modern life has driven man to a state where the rhythm of life is fast-growing erratic, and the music is slowly ebbing out. Living in a harsh world, we have developed cynicism and hatred. It would be wise to recall Imam Ghazali's description of Sufis: "Their knowledge aims to lop off the obstacles present in the soul and to rid oneself of its reprehensible habits and vicious qualities to attain thereby a heart empty of all save God and adorned with the constant remembrance of God."

The Sufis are moderate, tolerant, peace-loving and highly spiritual Muslims. They are light years away from the violent image of Islam projected by Western audiences. They believe God must always be at the forefront of one's thoughts. The *dhikr* rituals, which include dancing and religious songs, are aimed at nothing more than the remembrance of God. Why the government would want to ban a peaceful and harmless practice is incomprehensible.

In Egypt, Sufism is more institutionalised than anywhere else. There are 74 Sufi orders in Egypt, each headed by its own Sufi sheikh. At the top is a Supreme Council for Sufi Orders, and the president is directly in charge of Sufi affairs. Some Sufi orders are r 700 years old. Salafis have been fighting Sufis for ages. They accuse them of polytheism and unbelief for revering the Sufi sheikhs and building mosques at their shrines. They regularly call for the banning of all moulids(a term derived from the Arabic word meaning birth. It also refers to al Mawlid al-Nabawi, the celebration of the birthday of Prophet Muhammad) and *dhikr* ceremonies and succeeded in this respect last year when the moulid of al-Sayyida Zeinab, the prophet Muhammad's granddaughter, was banned.

The Sufi founders' shrines are in mosques, and millions of Muslims travel to them yearly to celebrate the birthdays (*moulids*) of the Sufi sheikhs and seek their blessings. The *dhikr* ceremonies and *moulids* have been cultural practices for centuries and are a part of Egypt's heritage. The *moulids* last for several days and are occasions for happiness, festivities, remembrance of God, charity for the impoverished and fun for children. Perhaps the spirituality of Sufism has been neglected by some in recent times. Still, the *dhikr* ceremonies and *moulids* have been cultural practices for centuries and are a part of Egypt's heritage. The *moulids* last for several days and are occasions for happiness, festivities, remembrance of God, income for the impoverished and fun for children.

Sufism's offer of a salve

The most authentic hope for a severe spiritual catharsis comes from mystics whose philosophy combines the virtuous message of formal religion with the intangible values of love and harmony. Rumi (which means daylight), the great 13th-century Sufi mystic, was the finest exponent of this luminous philosophy. Rumi sought freedom for his soul through a mystical connection with the divine. Not every wayfarer who sets out on the path may attain the goal, but for Rumi, the Sufi path offers the best potential for achieving actual knowledge.

Sufism is a mystical Islamic belief and practice in which Muslims seek to find the truth of divine love and knowledge through direct personal experience of God. It consists of various mystical paths designed to ascertain the nature of humanity and God and to facilitate understanding the presence of divine love and wisdom in the world. Sufism is the confluence of the noble virtues of all the great prophets of Islam. The all-pervading and tolerant spirit of the Sufis is not surprising when we consider their sources of inspiration. Although the Prophet Muhammad is their ultimate model, other spiritual figures – including Abraham, Moses, and Jesus – also mould them.

By educating the masses and deepening the spiritual concerns of the Muslims, Sufism has played an essential role in forming Muslim society. Opposed to the dry casuistry of the lawyer divines, the true mystics nevertheless scrupulously observed the commands of the divine law. The Sufis have elaborated on the image of the Prophet Muhammad and have thus primarily influenced Muslim piety by integrating his mysticism into their practices. Sufis believe the heart is the most crucial centre governing our spiritual consciousness. With diligent practice, teachers of Sufism perfected techniques that activate the heart, cultivating profound intuition and realization. The polished heart becomes a mirror that catches the light of truth and reflects it in one's consciousness.

Sufism offers direct access to God

A fundamental concept in Sufism is that seekers have direct access to God and can commune with Him. This inner celestial experience g could only be perceived and not communicated to others. An equally central notion is developing a person's potential to exalt a spiritual level of understanding. Sufis consider the spirit and body to be one whole. They believe in integration, not dichotomies. What we do physically affects us spiritually and vice versa. We cannot look at our lives in a vacuum. The critical element is the balance between the mundane and the divine. A well-known Sheikh Muzaffer says, "Keep your hands busy with your duties in this world and your heart busy with God." Our faith has to be practised daily within our everyday lives. As Sahi, an eminent Sufi mystic, urges: "A man should be in the marketplace while still working with true reality."

Ibn Khaldun, the 14th-century Arab historian, described Sufism as.".. dedication to worship, total dedication to Allah Most High, disregard for the finery and ornament of the world, abstinence from the pleasure, wealth, and prestige sought by most men, and retiring from others to worship alone." (Ibn Khaldun, quoted in Keller, Nuh Ha Mim, The Place of Tasawwuf in Traditional Islam, www.masud.co.uk, 1995)

Several Sufis feel that the time was approaching when their esoteric knowledge and defined contours of the unconscious, accumulated over centuries, would spread their trajectory to the West, a spiritual desert. Sufism is already leading the way in greening this aridity. While the West has been developing its technological prowess, the mystics have developed a sophisticated type of inner technology in their practices – a way of moving towards self-realization.

Historically, there are a couple of features of Sufism that rankle the fundamentalists. One is that Sufism, many feel, encourages a kind of fatalism and withdrawal from the realities of the world, which amounts to an escapist approach which can generate tendencies of monasticism. The second is that Sufism looks a little like Christianity. Sufis believe in intercessors (in Arabic, *wali* or *auliya'*)—people with special spiritual access who can help God hear a person's prayers. Mainstream Islam rejects intercessors since it holds that every Muslim is equal before God. (Even the prophet Muhammad is not prayed to but prayed for.)

Rumi-the great mystic poet

Rumi is an acclaimed mystic poet in the United States. He is a mystic, a saint, and an enlightened man. He was born into a religious family and followed the fundamental tenets of Islam, including daily prayer and fasting. Islam's acclaimed intellectual poet, Muhammad Iqbal, was a great admirer of Rumi but regarded Sufism as 'nullification respect of the search for 'inner meanings' or 'hidden meanings' in either the code of Prophet Muhammad or in his way of life, which he found not only satisfying but also convincing. He blamed the Persian poets for confusing the message of Islam. As he put it, "The Persian poets tried to undermine the way of Islam by a very roundabout, though apparently heart-alluring, manner. They made contemplation in a monastery the highest crusade in the way of God".

To Iqbal, the Hellenic–Persian mysticism was 'nihilism'. He observed: "Having lost the vitality to grapple with the temporal, these prophets of decay apply themselves to the quest of a supposed eternal, and gradually complete the spiritual impoverishment and physical degeneration of their society by evolving a seemingly charming ideal of life which reduces the healthy and powerful to death".

As he urges in his famous poem:

"Tu Shaheen Hai, Parwaz Hai Kaam Tera
Tere Samne Asman Aur Bhi Hain
Issi Roz-o-Shab Mein Ulajh Kar Na Reh Ja
Ke Tere Zaman-o-Makan Aur Bhi Hain"

(You are an eagle, flight is your vocation:
You have other skies stretching out before you.
Do not let mere day and night ensnare you,
Other times and places belong to you)

Though some Muslims may find Rumi and Sufism unorthodox, Rumi accepts the *shari'ah* but instead assumes that it is the rudiments of religion. He explains in the prose introduction to book five of the Masnavi, the *shari'ah* is like a candle that lights the way – without that candle, we cannot even see to set foot on the spiritual path. But once the law illuminates the path, the wanderer must begin the quest, and his walking along the way is the Sufi mode (*tariqa*). The goal of the pursuit is nothing short of truth (*haqiqa*).

Rumi's masterpiece, the *Masnavi*, is a six-book epic poem he wrote toward the end of his life. Its fifty thousand lines are mainly Persian but with Arabic excerpts from Muslim scripture. The work has been nicknamed the Persian Qur'an.). Rumi himself described the "Masnavi" as "the roots of the roots of the roots of religion"—meaning Islam—"and the explainer of the Qur'an." Yet, little trace of the religion exists in the translations that sell so well in the United States. Sadly, the translators have stripped the poetry of its Qur'anic ethos.

It is totally against Rumi's convictions. In an authentic quatrain composed by him, he tells us:

"I am the servant of the Qur'an as long as I have life.
I am the dust on the path of Muhammad, the Chosen one.
If anyone quotes anything except this from my sayings,
I am quit of him and outraged by these words."

(Rumi's Quatrain No. 1173, translated by Ibrahim Gamard and Ravan Farhadi in 'The Quatrains of Rumi')

To understand Rumi without the Qur'an is like reading Milton without the Bible. Even if Rumi was heterodox, it's essential to recognize that he was heterodox in a Muslim context—and that Islamic culture, centuries ago, had room for such heterodoxy. Rumi's works do not weave religion; they represent the historical dynamism within Islamic scholarship. Rumi advocated that an individual and interior spirituality and God's love, rather than fear, lie at the heart of his message. He attempts to merge the spirit of the human with the ideal of a god of love, whom Rumi locates within the human heart. Rumi's first biographer, Aflaki, tells of a man who came to Rumi asking how he could reach the other world, as only then would there be peace. "What do you know about where He is?" asked Rumi. "Everything in this or that world is within you.

A closer look at Sufism and Salafism

A simple definition of Sufism is in order. Imam al-Ghazali says of the Sufis: "Their knowledge aims to lop off the obstacles present in the soul and to rid oneself of its reprehensible habits and vicious qualities to attain thereby a heart empty of all save God and adorned with the constant remembrance of God." The Sufis are moderate, tolerant, peace-loving and highly spiritual Muslims, light years away from the violent image of Islam projected to Western audiences. They believe God must always be at the forefront of one's thoughts. The *dhikr* rituals, which include dancing and religious songs, are aimed at nothing more than the remembrance of God.

Salafism, imported into Egypt from Saudi Arabia and publicised around the world, is the enemy of anything moderate and tolerant. The Salafis believe that the only true path is to follow the practices of the early generations of Muslims. Salafi thinking has gradually occupied Egyptian thought over the past three decades, and it strongly emphasises the exterior beliefs and rituals as against the inner spirit. They grow their beards just as the first Muslims did and trim their trousers so that the hems hang well above the ankles (or wear a short jilbab), and their women usually wear the niqab. They believe that anything that deviates from their strictly literal interpretations of Islam is *bida'a* (innovation) and, thus, a gateway to hell. They indulge extensively in public displays of religiosity, such as beards, prayer beads, prayer calluses and women's clothing. At the same time, the spiritual aspect of religion and the proper ethics Muslims should adhere to take a back seat.

Western observers often associate Sufism with an acceptable, moderate, and enjoyable understanding of Islam. Indeed, Sufism in Egypt relates to a popular religion and beloved religious festivals. Politically, Sufi groups are allied with liberal parties or Egypt's moderate, pro-government religious establishment. It is unlikely, however, that the ubiquity of Sufism in Egyptian life would ever translate into political influence.

Sufism and Sufi organizations are either too much a part of Egyptian life to stand out as an identifying political motivator or too subservient to the state religious establishment to push for any dramatic change. Indeed, in the wake of the first round of elections, Sufi parties have been associated with old-regime elements. Unlike Western reactions when the word"Sharia" is invoked, the overwhelming majority of Egyptians associate the term with laudable ideals like social, political, and gender justice.

Salafism has leapt into salience since the revolution and has become one of the most effective mobilizers. Salafi political parties have been the most energetic, albeit controversial, parties. They now have a real stake in the democratic process. This development has caused great alarm in Egypt and among outside observers. Salafis' austere and uncompromising understanding of Islamic law and worship frightens many and raises palpable concerns about an Iranian-style theocracy. Such problems might lead some to conclude that opposing or repressing Salafi's political ambitions would be prudent.

The political suppression of Salafis would most likely prove unwise. Echoing the experience of Islamists in Turkey and of Salafis in Kuwait, actual involvement in an open democratic system leads to significant mitigation in Salafi positions. The need to mollify public concerns, engage women in the electoral process, and centralize political messaging has resulted in a rapid maturation and moderating discipline within Salafi ranks.

Egypt's aftershocks of the political tsunami continue to impact the daily alignments, re-alignments and coalition-building unfolding. The latest to enter the foray is the Sufis – at the invitation of the country's fragile liberal forces struggling to make an impact against the more solidified religious forces. There is no escape from religion in Egypt – post-revolution is more like pre-revolution. Copts and Muslims are equally spiritual and take the religious experience very seriously. It isn't easy to imagine Egypt without the Nile. Likewise, it is impossible to imagine Egypt without religion and religiosity.

In theory, liberal and secular recipes might have some value in them as templates of political correctness and modernising veneer. In practice, they are not enabling enough, at least not yet, for forces and voices espousing them to bite into the body politic.

Salafis regularly oppose Sufism as un-Islamic and their rituals as nullification of Islamic beliefs and regard their actions as amounting to infidelity. They also accuse them of encouraging sin and evil because the mixing of the sexes takes place at the shrines and during the moulids. Indeed, they do not enforce any strict segregation between men and women. Both sexes usually mix inside major mosques; the only separation occurs during prayer when women stand behind the men. Such mixing of the sexes is seen as pure evil by the Salafis and unacceptable by many Egyptians.

Incidentally, Sufism has become a kind of New-Age amalgam of spiritual practices, even though its roots reach back to the earliest days of Islam. The early Muslim conquerors took their faith to different lands. Sufism borrowed various traditions from Greek and Hindu philosophy and Christian theology. Many of the early Sufis believed that all religions were equal. It is here that Muslims believe that it was Sufism that went astray, and their faith got co; contaminated and vitiated the o; original concept of Islamic mysticism. astray. The way forward to explore a unifier effect for Sufism and Salafism was that Salafism could soften their stance, and Sufism could discipline their loose practices.

We can finally sum up Sufism in this lovely quote: "Today Sufism is a name without a reality. It was once a reality without a name."(Abu l-Hasan Fushanji, quoted in Lings, Martin, What is Sufism? The Islamic Texts Society, 1999,)This description can open a new path for the confluence of these two faiths, which have gradually diverged due to several misunderstandings. They remain tributaries of the same river.

* * * *

7. IT IS TIME TO REFOCUS OUR MENTAL AND SOCIAL LENS

At no stage in modern Indian history have Muslims been put to such a stern test. Their actions through a suspicious lens and even their positive contributions are perceived negatively or deftly airbrushed as insignificant. The mainstream narrative pigeonholes the entire community into stereotypical templates – that of fanatical, undisciplined, conspiratorial and unpatriotic Muslims.

Earlier, the right-wing media had labelled Muslims into two categories: good Muslims and bad Muslims. COVID-19 helped these religious anthropologists get over even that inconvenient distinction. Now, all Muslims are being straight-jacketed into a standard singular identity – that all Muslims are bad. They are all tarred as uniformly untrustworthy. Nobody wants to hear anything good about Muslims. Ears have grown deaf to such sentiments.

The propaganda machine works with such ferocious velocity that the voices of reason and logic are getting drowned in this high-voltage crescendo against Muslims. Positive examples, like the benevolent deeds of Muslim corporate houses like Cipla and Wipro and the Khan celebrities, are portrayed as isolated flashes of philanthropy. These pseudo-intellectuals detest the fact that Islamic monuments bear Muslim ties and resent that historians have documented facts about them so solidly that consistent attempts to efface their identity have not yielded any fruit.

Media, rights and injustice

At this juncture, we do not need revolutionary advocacy to explain how prejudiced, misinformed and misdirected the media is. Every age has witnessed such threats to pluralist societies, and the time-honoured message of our scriptures has enabled humanity to ride out these storms against our faith and keep the Muslim solidarity intact. We must revisit these scriptures and their original content to understand their divine message and distinguish them from invented religious thoughts and practices conjured by false assumptions about the faith circulated with ill intentions. However, for many adversaries, this image has become the more recognised face of all organized religions.

The divine books are the work of an infallible God, but human-mandated practices that have shrouded the original divine message are products of the minds of fallible human beings. It is the root cause of misunderstanding and the wrong beliefs that abound among adherents, most of whom are illiterate or incapable of comprehending the scriptures.

It is in these misgivings that we see a distorted worldview of Islam projected to the world. With the powerful influence of Islamophobic brigades, there has been a massive surge of hatred against Islam and its adherents. Muslims continue to be demonized and projected as uniformly fundamentalist and violent. This powerfully flawed narrative and negative stereotyping continue to fuel distorted perceptions about Islam. This portrayal lacks rigorous evidence or scientific inquiry but springs from biased reporting and misguided speculation in the media. In a climate where Muslims are already feeling alienated and marginalized, it is unfair to mock and ridicule their religion and identity.

In the last several decades, the judicial courts, in a few, have had the embarrassing situation of facing lawsuits that sought to delete certain verses of the Qur'an. There is a great deal of misunderstanding about the authentic message of the Qur'an. Verses are being cherry-picked and decontextualised by mischief-makers who wish to inflame passions, foster misunderstandings, and perpetuate violence.

First, as a Muslim, you are not supposed to alter the Qur'an because it is a revealed text. The spelling of its words, pronunciation, etc., also gives the Qur'an universality because it is the exact text worldwide. Therefore, we cannot just remove verses from the Qur'an. Indeed, a book has its unique context, and we need to understand it when reading it out of its context. It is so with the Qur'an nor with any other scriptures,

Islam is a massive faith with 1.6 billion followers spread across the Islamic world that stretches over 15,000 kilometres. A considerable section of the community lives as a minority community in many countries, battling issues of stereotyping, discrimination and identity. With the powerful influence of Islamophobic brigades, there has been a massive surge of hatred against Islam; Muslims continue to be demonized and projected as uniformly fundamentalist, violent and anti-secular. This powerfully flawed narrative and negative stereotyping continue to fuel Islam's distorted perceptions. This perception lies on rigorous evidence but springs from intermittent reporting and speculation in the media. In a climate where Muslims are already feeling alienated and marginalized, it is unfair to mock and ridicule their religion and identity.

Islam is a religion of peace: That is its aim and goal. The Qur'an's powerful commandment should leave one in no doubt: "Whosoever killeth a human being for other than manslaughter or corruption in the earth, it shall be as though he had killed all of mankind, and whoso saveth the life of one, it shall be as if he had saved the life of all mankind" (Q5:32). The Qur'an, in its essence, promotes justice, peace and freedom. Compassion and kindness underpin its core message. One must read the entire Qur'an, not isolated verses, to understand this. No verse in the Qur'an is a standalone commandment. Each not only has a bearing on the other but amplifies it, too.

The voice of the text is the fruit of a dialogue. For some, the peace of God is through his sword; for others, it lies in his unbounded mercy. The entire paradigm stands around human interpretation. The pacifists and the terrorists read the exact text but present fundamentally different interpretations. It is essential to consider the reader and interpreter of the Qur'an. The voice of the Qur'an heard by Islamic fundamentalists is not the same as the voice heard by progressive Muslims. The entire verses of the Qur" must be read and understood in conjunction with each other. Reading and interpreting verses in isolation is an incorrect way of engaging with the Qur'an. It would yield a meaning that conforms to one's worldview.

Islam shuns violence

For example, the current modern definition of striving spiritually or physically against evil is colloquial: religious war is contrary to the linguistic meaning of the word and also contrary to the beliefs of most Muslims who equate it with religious extremism. The word striving spiritually or physically against evil, colloquial: religious war, stems from the Arabic root word J-H-D, which means "strive." Other words derived from this root include "effort," "labour", and "fatigue." Essentially, striving spiritually or physically against evil; colloquial: religious war is a struggle to stand by one's religion in the face of oppression and persecution. The effort may be in fighting the evil in your heart or standing up to a dictator. It signifies a "resistance to oppression" (Q25:26) that is spiritual and intellectual rather than militant.

The moralist approach espouses striving spiritually or physically against evil; colloquial: religious war through conscience; striving spiritually or physically against evil; colloquial: religious war bin nafs), while a more radical wing advocates striving spiritually or physically against evil colloquial: religious war through the sword (striving spiritually or physically against evil; colloquial: religious war bin saif). In mainstream Muslim tradition, the greatest striving spiritually or physically against evil is colloquial: religious war was not warfare but reform of oneself and one's society. Prophet Muhammad explained that true striving spiritually or physically against evil, colloquial: religious war, was an inner struggle against egotism. There is a lot of misunderstanding because of this verse: "Slay them wherever you catch them" (Q2:191). But who is this referring to? Who are "they" that this verse discusses? The "them" are those terrorists who persecuted and killed innocent people for their faith. Some verses are very often "snipped" out of context by mischief makers for inflaming emotions, fostering misunderstandings and perpetuating violence on all sides. Qur'an 3:8 preemptively calls out people who cherry-pick verses as "perverse" people, declaring, "...those in whose hearts is perversity seek discord and wrong interpretation of [the Qur'an]."

The acts of violence against innocents transgress the fundamental tenets of the Islamic faith. And fellow citizens need to understand that. The English translation is not as eloquent as the original Arabic. We need to quote from the Qur'an to understand the more significant impact: In the long run, evil in the extreme will end those who do evil. For that, they rejected the signs of Allah and were subject to ridicule. The face of terror is not the true faith of Islam. That's not what Islam is all about. Islam is peace. These terrorists don't represent peace. They represent evil and war. When we think of Islam, we think of a faith that comforts millions worldwide. Billions of people find comfort, solace, and peace. And that's made brothers and sisters out of every race – out of every race.

Tolerance is the essence of Islam

On his victorious rerun to Mecca after 20 years, the Prophet Muhammad bore no hatred for the locals who had persecuted him and his band, forcing them to emigrate to Medina. He offered blanket forgiveness, the only condition being that Meccans accept universal freedom of conscience. In keeping with this spirit of tolerance that Prophet Muhammad demonstrated during his lifetime, today's Muslim thinkers feel there exists no imperative to distance themselves from this tradition of mutual respect and peaceful coexistence. They are plumbing it to find resources to help them adapt to the modern world and to shape it on those lines. Muslim religious scholars are exhuming and popularizing principles and practices that allowed Muslims in the past to coexist with others in peace and on equal terms, regardless of creed and faith. They keep reminding themselves that the seventh-century Medina accepted Jews as equal members of the community (umma) under the Constitution of Medina drawn up by Prophet Muhammad in 622 A.D.

Muslim reformers are returning to the foundational text, the Qur" and its commentaries and other early sources of religion – authentic sayings of Prophet Muhammad and early historical chronicles – to seek solutions in these troubled times. They are combing their literature to shed better light on moral guidelines and ethical prescriptions. There is no better testament to Prophet Muhammad's philosophy of tolerance and forgiveness than the attestation of non-Muslim historian Stanley Lane-Poole: "The day of Muhammad's greatest triumph over his enemies was also the day of his grandest victory over himself. He freely forgave the Quraysh all the years of sorrow and cruel scorn they had afflicted him and gave an amnesty to the whole population of Mecca."

The core messages

The voice of the text is the fruit of a dialogue. For some, the peace of God is through his sword; for others, it lies in his unbounded mercy. The entire paradigm stands around human interpretation. The pacifists and the terrorists read the exact text but present fundamentally different interpretations. It is essential to consider the reader and interpreter of the Qur'an. The voice of the Qur" heard by Islamic fundamentalists is not the same as the voice heard by progressive Muslims.

All the verses of the Qur'an must be read and understood in conjunction with each other. Reading and interpreting verses in isolation is an incorrect way of engaging with the text. Much of the strife and misunderstanding of the scripture is primarily on account of selective reading and lacks reference to the context of the verses.

For example, the current modern definition of *jiihad* considers it as striving spiritually or physically against evil, and this definition is closely related to the word " Islam ", which is repeatedly known as a religion of peace. That is its aim and goal. The Qur" an's powerful commandment should leave one in no doubt: "Whosoever killeth a human being for other than manslaughter or corruption in the earth, it shall be as though he had killed all of mankind, and whoso saveth the life of one, it shall be as if he had saved the life of all mankind" (Q5:32). The Qur'an", in essence, promotes justice, peace, equality, brotherhood, and freedom. Compassion and kindness underpin its core message. To understand this, one must read the Quran and not isolated verses. No verse is a standalone commandment. Each not only has a bearing on the other but amplifies it, too. The Qur'an is an integrated book, and egalitarianism is its underlying philosophy.

Religious war is contrary to the linguistic meaning of the word and also contrary to the beliefs of most Muslims who equate it with religious extremism. The word striving spiritually or physically against evil, colloquial: religious war, stems from the Arabic root word "J-H-D," which means "strive." Other words derived from this root include "effort," "labour" and "fatigue." Essentially, striving spiritually or physically against evil; colloquial: religious war is a struggle to stand by one's religion in the face of oppression and persecution. The effort may come in fighting the evil in your heart or standing up to a dictator.

Islam shuns violence

There is a lot of misunderstanding because of this verse: "Slay them wherever you catch them" (Q2:191). But who is this referring to? Who are "they" in this verse? The "them" are terrorists who persecuted and killed innocent people for their faith. Some verses are very often "snipped" out of context by mischief makers for inflaming emotions, fostering misunderstandings and perpetuating violence on all sides. Qur'an 3:8 preemptively calls out people who cherry-pick verses as "'perverse' people, declaring. .. those in whose hearts is perversity seek discord and wrong interpretation of (the Qur'an)." Islam does permit fighting but only in self-defence, in defence of religion or on the part of those who have been expelled forcibly from their homes.

The first time the word occurs in the Qur'an is in its significance to a "resistance to oppression" (Q25:26) that is spiritual and intellectual rather than militant. The moralist approach espouses striving spiritually or physically against evil, colloquial religious war through conscience (striving spiritually or physically against evil colloquial: religious war bin naïfs), while a more radical wing advocates striving spiritually or physically against evil; colloquial: religious war through the sword (striving spiritually or physically against evil; colloquial: religious war bin saif). In mainstream Muslim tradition, the actual meaning of *jehad* was not a military war but the most incredible spiritual or physical against evil. Its colloquial connotation implies reform of oneself and one's society and an inner struggle against egotism.

There are several caveats even concerning warfare in self-defence. First, Muslims cannot preemptively initiate a war. They are only allowed to act in defence. We can resort to wars in a situation where defenceless people are under attack. A war is when one party does not cease aggression despite a proposed truce. Muslims must follow suit if the enemy inclines toward peace: "But if they stop, God is most forgiving, most merciful" (Q2:192). Also read, "Now if they incline toward peace, then incline to it, and place your trust in God, for God is the all-hearing, the all-knowing" (Q8:61).

Second, Muslims are not allowed to transgress divine injunctions: "Fight for the cause of God, those who fight you, but do not transgress, for God does not love the transgressors." (Q2:190). Third, Muslims have to treat prisoners of war with honour. Prisoners must be set free after the war, either in exchange for Muslim captives or only as a favour.

Historian Sir William Muir records how the Prophet Muhammad instructed his companions to treat prisoners of war. The refugees had their own houses and received the prisoners with kindness and consideration. "Blessings on the men of Medina!" said one of them later: "They made us ride while they walked afoot; they gave us wheaten bread to eat when there was little of it, contenting themselves with dates."

Contrary to what some historians have portrayed, Islam did not impose itself by the sword. It has been emphatically made clear in the Qur'an: "There must be no coercion in matters of faith!" (Q2:256). In words quoted by Muhammad in one of his last public sermons, God tells all human beings: "O people! We have formed you into nations and tribes so that you may know one another" (Q49:13). Moreover, Islamic wars weren't just to defend Muslims against persecution but to defend Christians, Jews and people of all faiths. The Qur'an says that "persecution is worse than slaughter" and "let there be no hostility except to those who practice oppression" (Q2:190-193).

Tolerance is the essence

On his victorious rerun to Mecca after 20 years, the Prophet Muhammad bore no vengeance for the locals who had persecuted him and his band, forcing them to emigrate to Medina. He offered blanket forgiveness, the only condition being that Meccans accept universal freedom of conscience. In keeping with this spirit of tolerance that the Prophet Muhammad demonstrated during his lifetime, today's Muslim thinkers feel there exists no imperative to distance themselves from this tradition of mutual respect and peaceful coexistence. They are plumbing it to find resources to help them adapt to the modern world and shape it on those lines. Muslim religious scholars are exhuming and popularizing principles and practices that allowed Muslims in the past to coexist with others in peace and on equal terms, regardless of creed and faith. They keep reminding themselves that seventh-century Medina accepted Jews as equal members of the community (umma) under the Constitution of Medina drawn up by the Prophet Muhammad in 622.

Muslim reformers are returning to the foundational text, the Qur'an and its commentaries and other early sources of religion – authentic sayings of Prophet Muhammad and early historical chronicles – to seek solutions in these troubled times. They are combing their literature to shed better light on moral guidelines and ethical prescriptions. There is no better testament to the Prophet Muhammad's philosophy of tolerance and forgiveness than the attestation of non-Muslim historian Stanley Lane-Poole: "The day of Muhammad's greatest triumph over his enemies was also the day of his grandest victory over himself. He freely forgave the Quraysh all the years of sorrow and cruel scorn they had afflicted him and gave an amnesty to the whole population of Mecca."

In the above light, we must reshape our response to the current pandemic. We all now know that the COVID-19 pandemic was the culmination of our prolonged warfare that has tinctured the fabric of our planet. It is not just chemical warfare but warfare in its broadest manifestation that has brought us to the edge of this catastrophe. All forms of warfare, including warfare of religions and ideologies, are symptomatic of sick minds that need patient healing. It can understood when we renew our understanding of the insights of history and civilizations. These lessons dominate the founding philosophy of UNESCO, proclaiming that since wars begin in men's minds, the bulwarks of peace must find their roots. The minds of men will need to purge them of all sorts of misinformation being purveyed in the name of religion by self-appointed custodians. We need to understand every religion from its primary scriptures and not from secondary sources, which are prone to many misinterpretations and usually represent a particular school of thought. The only lasting solution will be to liberate society from artificial religion and return to the pristine message of the scriptures. These scriptures had a simple, straightforward and plain-speaking message for all humanity, which got distorted at the hands of the modern tools of intellectual sophistry and sterile polemics. We need to sanitize not just our bodies and our environment but also our minds and intellect.

We have bared religion of its humanist content, compassion, righteousness, tolerance and fairness and reduced it to a rigid set of social codes and practices considered the only valid credentials for attaining salvation. Fake religious leaders have adopted the responsibility of collective salvation, freeing humanity of its own individual moral and spiritual accountability. We must think and act at our level and abandon this trend of seeking salvation in herds to achieve our moral redemption. It is the distilled essence of all divine revelations. Our fight against COVID-19 was not an option. It was an imperative cause that needed absolute unity of purpose and complete trust among all humankind.

It is excruciating that some people continue to underscore imagined communal divergence in this dark hour, making us wonder about our fundamental objectives. Whatever the purveyors of hate might think they are achieving through the toxicity of their discourse, they do not realize they are causing irreversible damage to civil values.

Spiritual lessons of the pandemic

COVID-19 provided many spiritual lessons, apart from medical and biological lessons. One is that we have to be compassionate with our planet. But to achieve this, we must learn to be compassionate with ourselves and our brothers. We must be our brother's keeper. We must not forget that we are one species, Homo sapiens, and our planet is our common heritage. That is also the way to a more balanced, inclusive and equitable society. Being patient and composed in tough times is hard, especially when your personal and professional life is at stake. It requires much more resilience than most humans are built or trained for. Taking refuge in Islamic meditation and gaining emotional strength helped me. At the heart of self-consciousness in Islam is the idea of Nafs Mutmaen, a soul at ease with the body. It is possible to not corrupt your soul with lies and selfishness and to ensure you are always kind to others. Of course, one can argue that there would be no need for this if we lived in a perfect world without wars, poverty or political meddling. But is there such a thing as an ideal world? We shouldn't give up on striving for a better world where things are fair, transparent and accessible for all. But there are moments here and there when we need extraordinary interventions in our lives for good, and there is no harm or embarrassment in it.

History tells us that politics is vicious when there is a clash between beliefs and truth. Society has paid a heavy price for allowing politics to have its sway. We should grow wiser from the lessons of history. Let history not repeat itself. Let us not play with precious human lives.

* * * * *

8. MUSLIM WOMEN RECLAIM GENDER SPACE

"Learn this now and learn it well, my daughter: Like a compass needle that points north, a man's accusing finger always finds a woman. Always." In Khaled Hosseini's novel about life in Afghanistan, A Thousand Splendid Suns, the character Nana, a impoverished, unwed mother, gives this grim advice to her five-year-old daughter, Mariam. In 25 words, she tries to sum up how the world thinks men govern women's lives in the world of Islam.

The grim picture

The pictures of Muslim women that we glimpse in the media are grim and sombre. The public perception of them is one of stubborn stereotypes: supposedly powerless and oppressed, behind walls and veils, demure, voiceless and silent figures, discriminated against and bereft of even fundamental rights. The picture keeps reinforcing itself, mainly because this is how the Western media caricatures women in Islam. Recurring images beamed into our homes and phones keep strengthening the belief that Muslim women do not have access to education, social space, privacy and educational and development programmes for socio-economic uplift. But it has also reduced Muslim women to a stereotyped singularity, plastering a handy cultural icon over much more complicated historical and political dynamics. But in many cases, women are victims of prejudice and persecution. The ultimate truth of the plight of Muslim women was deceptively simple: the understanding of Muslim men about their status in the Qur'an was flawed.

For years, the vision of the transformation of Muslim women appeared hopelessly naïve. Their plight flowed primarily under the radar of Muslim rulers. It seemed to many observers that the dream had died; all that was left was to bury it. However, there were so many chance encounters that these women utilised to convert them into potential opportunities. Of the many tropes that have cluttered policy analysis in recent decades, few are as widespread or as enduring as the inevitability of the rise of Muslim women. In many Arab countries and Iran, more women attend university than men. However, it is now clear that the role of women in Muslim society has changed significantly in the centuries since Islam began in Arabia in the early 600s. Their position has varied with shifting social, economic, and political circumstances. Although Islam regards men and women as moral equals in the sight of God, women have not had equal access to many areas of Islamic life.

Today, solutions exist to solve some of women's most complex challenges. However, these solutions never reach women at the last mile to enable fundamental transformation in female society. We need to drive real change and shape concrete outcomes for our repressed females. We must balance risks and opportunities so they can perform multiple roles with more remarkable equipment to scale new solutions and innovations. It is the way they can push the envelope.

It is true that in societies trapped in poverty, illiteracy and ignorance, women continue to receive abominable and oppressive treatment. But then, this is true of all societies. Muslims cannot be singular victims of such a flawed social order. The pictures we get of wife beating and other retrograde practices imposed on Muslim women are aberrations which the usual Muslim stereotype should not undermine. The wrong practices rampant in some such societies have much to do with illiteracy, ignorance and sometimes dire poverty.

In several cases, the plight of Muslim women is a direct consequence of a repressive and highly discriminatory State. A dispassionate analysis will reveal that vested interests in all societies, mainly those driven by patriarchal values, have resisted the uplift of women and have failed to concede to them the legitimate rights given by their faith, community and the State.

This distortion, however, should not deflect our focus from some pathbreaking and stellar contributions of Muslim women, not just to Islamic civilisation but to secular society as well.

A most unforeseen development of modern history is the positive transformation of Muslim women. The women are not shunned by Muslim men nor prohibited from areas that are purely Muslim domains. Muslim women are no longer consenting to embrace a restrictive, seemingly sexist religious lifestyle. It is possible to reclaim the positive messages in the Qur'an and Islamic history and devise some Muslim feminism.

Liberal women are no longer an endangered species. The brightest hope for positive developments in this direction comes from black chadors of devout Iranian women who are camouflaging themselves and whose unquestioning adherence to religious rules gives them high ground to present their case for women's rights. They have used that position sparingly. Across South Asia, they are slowly becoming resilient through skill development and livelihood generation to stand up to patriarchal practices undermining their dignity in literate societies. We must give them sufficient leeway to pursue their objectives.

The performance of these women is no longer suboptimal, nor do they remain confined to being part of the supportive structure for men. Muslim women are an empowered community like their counterparts in other creeds. Several women are encouraging their philanthropic husbands to channel and expand the reach of capital into women's menstrual hygiene products targeted at feminine hygiene among women from low-income households to bring transformative impact in their lives. Women entrepreneurs amplify their marketing reach for low-cost, women-friendly products for overall hygiene to create more impact outcomes.

Qur'an's concept of the status of women

The Qur'an enshrined a new status for women and gave them rights that they could have only dreamed of before in Arabia, so why the seeming disparity between what once was and what now appears to be? The answer lies in the deterioration of primary Islamic education that occurred in the Muslim world after the disasters of the Mongol invasions and the Crusades in the eleventh through thirteenth centuries. The patrilineal traditions in the Middle East that preceded Islam both improved and curtailed women's freedoms in its earliest days. Much of the blame for the most constrictive interpretations of Islam is a product of the Abbasid dynasty, which ruled from the mid-eighth century onward and interpreted Islam in a legalistic and rigid manner designed to serve state interests, thereby sacrificing much of the ethical, normative thrust of the religion as practised in the days of Prophet Muhammad.

Historically, Islam was incredibly advanced in providing revolutionary rights for women and uplifting women's status in the seventh century. Many of the revelations in the Qur'an were by nature reform-oriented, transforming critical aspects of pre-Islamic customary laws and practices in progressive ways to eliminate injustice and suffering. Still, it is not enough to merely flaunt these values. We must act on them. The battle is with ideas, debate and scholarship. But most of all, it is being propelled by Muslim women. The reason is not hard to find. Over the centuries, women have been the first religious teachers in all Muslim homes. If women define and implement a new dispensation for themselves, society begins to change at its most basic level. In due course, this revolution engulfs society and permeates every sphere.

Cultures that arose since then have been characterized by customs and localized leanings more than genuine Islamic values. The lives of the first Muslim women represent valuable models, transcending time and physical boundaries; therefore, these models can serve as powerful, culturally authentic tools in advancing the human rights agenda toward increased female empowerment in the political, social and economic spheres in Muslim communities. The contributions of these women to the Muslim community are undeniable; to some, they even appear almost mythical. They are mistakenly subscribing to the erroneous notion that contemporary Muslim women cannot attain such stature. However, these women represent others who lived, fought, learned, worked and led during Islam's foundational period and beyond. Their male companions, the caliphs who assumed Muslim rule following the demise of Prophet Muhammad, treated them with respect, admiration and appreciation as equals. Society needs to pursue female society's progress actively; otherwise, complacency can lead to regression.

In the twentieth century, the combined spread of literacy, the availability and promotion of public education for both girls and boys, the expansion of job opportunities for women, and the rising number of conversions to Islam from other religious traditions, particularly in the West, have added to the desire of Muslim women for greater empowerment in the practice and interpretation of their faith.

Muslim women have proven resourceful, creative, and dedicated to claiming ownership of and responsibility for their faith individually and communally. It is despite the challenges they have often faced in gaining access to the appropriate religious training facilities and establishing credibility with the male religious establishment, particularly conservatives. Today, Muslim women are active in Qur'anic study circles, mosque-based activities, community services sponsored by religious organizations, and Islamic education as students and teachers. There are a rising number of female Qur'an reciters, Islamic lawyers, and professors of Islamic studies. This dynamism has found a pair in their commitment to building a healthy and cultured family.

Colonial era's deep scars on women

It has become trite to say that Muslim women are facing persecution. There are several reasons for this assumption. The colonial era has undoubtedly left deep scars, but we must understand that rejecting the West and criticizing it for the shortcomings of our world cannot be a seductive and easy way out. Instead, the gaze should now turn inward. Muslims need to look at themselves realistically instead of their imagined selves. The prophet was centuries ahead of the men of his time in his attitudes toward women, and not surprisingly, right after he died, men started rolling back his reforms. The prophet may have been too advanced for the mindset of seventh-century men, but his compassion for women is the model that Muslims in the 21st century need to emulate today.

Even in those nascent stages, Islam sought to elevate women and define them as independent agents of free will. Twenty-four women appear in the Qur'an in various forms and for multiple purposes; 18 of those women appear as minors, the primary five being: Mary, mother of Jesus, Bilquis, the queen of Sheba, Mary's mother Hannah, Hawa (Eve) and Umm Musa, the mother of Moses. All of them are potent examples of the tremendous potential of women.

Women empowerment

Contemporary Muslim women's activism in claiming an interpretive role within the Islamic tradition focuses on three key aspects of religious life: Reciting, teaching and interpreting the Qur'an. There is a diversity of voices in debates concerning a more empowering role for women, some conservative, others self-designated "progressive," who claim an equal position for both sexes and others affirming specific unique roles for men and women. Vibrant, passionate and often contentious, these debates are among the most important in defining Islam and the place of women in it in the 21st century.

Although there have been significant strides in including women's voices in Islamic debates, challenges remain, particularly in widely accepted conservative interpretations that appear to be supported by Qur'anic texts. Muslim women have successfully networked and engaged in global dialogue and cooperation with other women. However, the ultimate success of joining women's voices to the interpretation of Islam requires their acceptance as equally capable interpreters alongside their male colleagues. Many Muslim men support and encourage this dialogue within Islam as critical to the development of Islam in the 21st century.

The elevation of the status of Muslim women

In Egypt, women comprise a more significant percentage of engineering and medical faculties than in the US. It is true that in societies trapped in poverty, illiteracy and ignorance, women continue to receive abominable and oppressive treatment. But then, this is true of all societies. Muslims are not solitary victims of such a flawed social order. This distortion, however, should not deflect our focus from some path-breaking and stellar contributions of Muslim women not just to Islamic civilization but to secular society as well. They have been instrumental in rolling out several unique initiatives. The freedom has complemented their concerted efforts in several fields conceded to them by several male societies. The women have already pushed the envelope so far and are certainly on the cusp of a gradually evolving revolution. There have been sincere efforts to bring more diverse yet unique perspectives and unearth fresh ideas to synthesise the existing approaches of women in nurturing ecosystems to deliver change.

In the 21st century, the combined spread of literacy, the availability and promotion of public education for both girls and boys, the expansion of job opportunities for women and the rising number of conversions to Islam from other religious traditions, particularly in the West, have added to the desire of Muslim women for greater empowerment in the practice and interpretation of their faith.

As in other areas of life, Muslim women have proven to be resourceful, creative and dedicated to claiming ownership and responsibility for their faith individually and communally. It is in the face of challenges they have often faced in gaining access to the appropriate religious training facilities and establishing credibility with the male religious establishments. We are witnessing the onset of a new Muslim feminist revolution. Their unsavoury past is now far behind.

Today, Muslim women are active in Qur'anic study circles, mosque-based activities, community services sponsored by religious organizations, and Islamic education as students and teachers. There is a rising number of female Qur'an reciters, Islamic lawyers and professors of Islamic studies worldwide. This process also helps to shake up some traditionally held cultural misconceptions. All Muslims can further activate the reform process by re-examining the lives of the very first Muslim women who lived during Islam's formative period, not just as historical figures but as modern Islamic models. While many Muslims around the world learn about such exceptional Muslim women in school, their relevance to the contemporary context is undetermined. Most critical aspects of their life have not been kept alive. Through learning and celebrating their examples, men and women can better understand and build upon notions of the role of Muslim women in a culturally authentic paradigm.

The empowerment of Muslim women

Muslim women, like their counterparts in other creeds, are an empowered community. They believe that women were endowed d with enough rights in foundational Islamic texts, but that interpretation of these documents with the prevalent cultural lens disallows what is rightfully theirs. They do not call this a feminist struggle but describe it as a reclamation of their faith. The tragic irony of Islam is that the Qur'an is mainly concerned with women's well-being and development, yet Islamic traditions discriminate against girls. The Qur'anic description of marriage suggests closeness, mutuality, and equality, but tradition defines a husband as his wife's god in earthly terms. The Qur'an provides rights that address the common complaints of women, such as the lack of freedom to make decisions for themselves and the inability to earn an income.

The challenge for all women, and especially Muslim women, is to move from a reactive mindset, in which women must assert their autonomy over patriarchal opposition, to a proactive attitude, in which they can speak of themselves as full and independent human beings with minds and spirits as well as bodies. Central to Islamic belief is the importance and high value placed on education. From the valid Islamic point of view, education should be freely and equally available to women as much as men. Today, several women have distinct outlooks, and their ideas are no longer behind the times. They have dramatic and completely diverse interests, values, and perspectives, which sets them apart from men.

Muslim women have surmounted many complex challenges, and several of them have assumed strategic roles in giant corporations and have been instrumental in handling several vital political roles. Although traditionally excluded from the male public domain, Muslim women are now privately involved in the study and oral transmission of Islamic source texts (the Qur'an and Hadith). In modern times, they have entered both secular and religious forms of education with enthusiasm, supporting their long-standing role as family educators and moral exemplars, as well as training for professional careers in the workplace outside the home. The Muslim women are now an empowered community, and no deterrent can make them retreat from this[position of strength.

Islamic scholar Sheikh Mohammad Akram Nadwi's epic work al-Muhaddithat: The Women Scholars in Islam stands as a riposte to the notion, peddled from Jakarta to Morocco, that Islamic knowledge is men's work and always has been. "I do not know of another religious tradition in which women were so central, so present, so active in its formative history," Akram writes.

Muslim women now believe that Islamic texts give rights but that cultural interpretations of these same texts disallow what is rightfully theirs. They do not call this a feminist struggle but describe it as a reclamation of their faith. Their emancipatory readings of foundational Islamic texts reveal Muslim women's activism around education and equal opportunities.

They are also challenging the elements of patriarchy that all women experience around unequal power hierarchies in society. Similarly, they are protesting and influencing their cou; counterparts in other religions against the objectification of women's bodies in some sections of the media. These women have been able to realign their roles and efficiently optimize their outcomes and impacts.

Social values strongly reinforce orientation towards marriage and children as the normative pattern based on Prophet Muhammad's example. Childrearing, early education, and socialisation of children are among the most important tasks for women in Islamic societies worldwide. Although traditionally excluded from the public male domain, Muslim women are privately involved in the study and oral transmission of Islamic source texts (the Qur'an and Hadith). In modern times, they have entered both secular and religious forms of education and continue to support their long-standing role as family educators and moral exemplars. Muslim women are now exploring diverse fields. They are flocking to higher education institutions as their guardians sincerely invest in their education. They continue bearing the triple burden of livelihood, child-rearing, cooking and nursing those in the family who are ill.

Several Muslim women are successful entrepreneurs and have inspired bustling hubs of businesses. Education is a Muslim women's activist tool, and they have leveraged it very usefully. It is essentially a product of the hybridisation of education and business training. Despite facing a steep learning curve, Muslim women have been equal to the challenges and have surmounted the handicaps and attained higher grades in education. Central to Islamic belief is the importance and high value placed on education. From a valid Islamic point of view, education should be freely and equally available to women as much as men. Islam has anticipated and activated the vision of Western feminists for their women for more than 1,000 years. A stay-at-home wife can specify that she expects to receive a regular stipend, which is not that far from the goals of the Wages for Housework campaign of the 1970s.

Elsewhere, the fully empowered Muslim woman sounds like a self-assured, post-feminist type, a woman who draws her inspiration from the example of Sukayna, the brilliant, beautiful great-granddaughter of the Prophet Muhammad. She was married several times and, at least in one of her marriages, stipulated in writing that her husband was forbidden to disagree with her about anything. All these conditions rely on the canons of Islam and early Muslim practice. A Muslim woman cannot enter into marriage without her co; consent t; indeed, she has the right to revoke a marriage to which she did not agree in the first place.

Muslim women overshadow their Western counterparts

A comparison may mean little outside the cultural context, but it is essential to point out that, until 100 years ago, western women had virtually no rights in law or practice. Over 1,000 years before the first

European suffragette, Islam gave women far-reaching rights and a defined status. However, these Western attitudes have undoubtedly helped to stimulate discussions of the problem in Muslim urban society, thereby revealing the gap between the talk of the Islamic ideal and the actual situation of women.

Women emerged as the centrepiece of the Western narrative of Islam in the 19th century and, notably, in the later 19th century as Europeans established themselves as colonial powers in Muslim countries. Their narratives simultaneously and hypocritically perpetuated the Victorian English narrative that European men were superior to women while denigrating Muslim culture for being oppressive to women.

Muslim women certainly do not share the Western notion of feminism. These women do not accept that being feminist means being Western and emphasise that Western women should be respectful of other paths to social change. First of all, there are multiple causes of discrimination against women, and religion is but one. Secondly, gender relations explain women's options in all societies. Thirdly, it is futile to focus on misery elsewhere as an escape from the realities of our own lives. Fourth, the issue of power remains crucial for understanding gender inequality in any society.

We now have a curious and empowered generation that will not easily accept rules and codes without reasoning and arguing on every strand before embracing them. A heartening development is that, unlike earlier times, when only those who had finally retired from all worldly responsibilities would make the hajj pilgrimage, the youth actively participates in this most potent Islamic exercise.

Hajj is a revolutionary experience that radically transforms one's mindset and provides a correct perspective of Islam. Exposure to a composite global culture gives a refreshing perspective to the pilgrim. Few Muslim women outside the urban areas may want to behave like Western women. The high rate of divorce and sexual disease are expected consequences of the reckless drive to equate the sexes and "free" sexual relationships.

Life and opportunities are now unfolding for Muslim women. Women are now elbowing their way into politics, civil society, and universities. Despite present cultural and political obstacles, they are finding opportunities to rise – and to bring their societies up with them. They feel the key is to do so within Islamic paradigms. We now have female politicians, journalists, entrepreneurs, and educators, both urban and rural, who are making impressive inroads.

Western thinkers and practitioners must reconsider their assumptions about the role of Islam in women's rights and approach this topic with a more nuanced lens. They must understand the necessity of recognising and consciously accepting the broad cultural differences between Western and non-Western conceptions of autonomy and respecting social standards that reflect non-Western values. Western societies must be sensitized to make informed decisions and initiate appropriate interventions as far as Muslim female society is concerned.

Muslim women maintain a respectful distance from males as a part of their modesty, but that does not compel them to retreat from their vibrant dynamism. They are no longer victims of timidity and have overcome their earlier vulnerability to prejudicial social norms. They also often shrug off the disrespectful annoyance of strangers. They were once quite hesitant and reticent but are now swift and decisive in their life. They have sparked their inner abilities and are pushing the frontiers of possibilities.

The controversy around women's dress

Women's dress is a favourite subject of religious bigots of all hues with their notions of morality. Everyone wants to talk about the "moral values" attached to women's dress or the "purity" of their attire that "go against the parameters" laid down by the moral police. Nobody is interested in discussing the more critical issue—the morality or purity of one's conscience. Today, a woman's character is identified d by her clothes. Natural markers like piety and morality have lost their relevance.

Modesty is a virtue for both men and women. A connection between spiritual life and modesty exists because that virtue is not just about outward appearances. Instead, it is tolerance, first and foremost, about the inward state of having modesty before God – an awareness of divine presence everywhere and at all times that leads to propriety (within oneself and in one's most private moments). Outward modesty means behaving in a way that maintains one's self-respect and the respect of others, whether in dress, speech or behaviour. Inward modesty means shying away from any character or quality offensive to God.

When it comes to women's clothes, everybody seems to be obsessed with them. More than a means to cover one's body, women's clothes have become a symbol of oppression for some and a mark of liberation for others. But, more peculiarly, garments are often used as a benchmark by conservative Muslims to judge the morality of a Muslim woman and her "Muslimness". There is still no such benchmark for Muslim men who owe a duty of modesty to the Qur'an, whose injunctions are as vital for men as they are for women. Indeed, judging by the discourse, one would assume that the primary religious duty of Muslim women is to observe "the dress code".

In the context of proper attire and conduct, the Qur'an forbids modesty on men, too and only when the men have attained that level of modesty should they feel justified in talking about the modesty of others. "Tell the believing men to lower their gaze (avoiding its concentration on a person's body, or a certain part of it) and to be mindful of their chastity; in this, they will be more considerate for their well-being and purity, and surely God is fully aware of all that they do (Q24: 30-31)."

From certain imams insisting that earthquakes are caused by women not wearing proper dresses to muftis excommunicating Muslim women, the intellectual level of discourse that surrounds Muslim women is excruciating and is more or less concerned only with notions of modesty. By reducing Muslim women to their bodies and pretending that modesty is their primary religious duty, we strip them of their personhood.

In the view of the great liberal Islamic scholar Mohammad Asad, what the Qur'an requires of women is that they should be clothed "decently". Elaborating on this point, he states: "My interpolation of the word 'decently' reflects the interpretation of the phrase 'illa ma zahara minha' by several of the earliest Islamic scholars, and particularly by Al-Qiffal (quoted by Razi, one of Islam's greatest high priests), as 'that which a human being may openly show following prevailing custom (al-'adah al-jariyah)'."

Today's world is in a state of great upheaval. With gnawing problems such as superstition, sectarianism, bigotry, sectarianism, and patriarchy in Muslim-majority states, we cannot afford to divert all our attention to pedantic details of how to worship God "correctly". If we are at all serious about preventing the so-called fitna (spiritual affliction), we must start addressing the real issue that has long been glaring at us—the attitude towards women.

Islam's idea of modesty

The shift in focus of religion from an ethical guide to policing of appearances (dress codes, rituals) is a curious phenomenon. This virus seems to have seeped its way into mainstream Muslim consciousness. Our religious priorities have shifted from spiritual transformation to quotidian concerns about rituals and dress codes. This fixation reflects the very cursory manner in which we approach religion.

Education, as always, is the key here. Let's start getting offended by expressions like "men will be men" because men are not monolithic sexual beasts who have no autonomy over their desires. Let's not tie down a woman's morality to her dress. And let's stop objectifying women and seeing them primarily as avenues for consumerism.

One of the Islamic symbols that has been attracting so much attention in the Western world is the veil – the hijab (a scarf wrapped tightly around a woman's head to conceal every wisp of hair). Veiling has become, perhaps more than any other single issue, the defining "women's question".

The hijab has now become the most potent symbol of Muslim women's rejection of Western notions of feminism. These empowered and educated women use the hijab to articulate a new response to modernity. The hijab also expresses a translational form of Islamic feminism marked by the entry of women into all public spheres of Islamic life, including formal religious learning.

The Western discourse has consistently argued that the hijab is not a symbol of freedom but one of oppression. It believes that women in Islam are second-class citizens and that this status is encoded in both sacred text and tradition, enforced by culture and law. If you browse the Western media's news stories, polls, and studies, they constantly strip the activity of a Muslim woman down to her hijab or attire. Have we forgotten that less than 100 years ago, American women did not have the freedoms and access that we now take for granted and promote as universal human rights?

Contrary to Western notions, Muslim women choose to wear the hijab as a way of showing self-control, power and agency. For example, many well-educated women working in hospitals and libraries wear it. They wear it not as a symbol of control by a man but rather to promote their feminist ideals. For many Muslim women, wearing a hijab offers a way for them to take control of their bodies and challenge how men marginalise women. They justify wearing the hijab as a public statement of their spiritual quest.

Veiling was once an armour for the impoverisheder classes. Today, it is the mascot of the most enlightened Muslim girls pursuing prestigious courses in top-class universities. Attempts to force Muslim women to stop wearing the veil might, therefore, be counterproductive by depriving them of the choice and opportunity to integrate. Women who cannot signal their piety by wearing a veil might choose to stay at home. Prophet Muhammad said, "Every religion has a chief characteristic, and the chief characteristic of Islam is modesty."

The Arabic word for modesty is *hayaa*. The exciting thing about this word is that it is linguistically related to the Arabic word for life (hayat). Muslim scholars and sages have taken from this that there is an intimate connection between the two terms. Modesty, it is said, is the virtue that gives spiritual life to the soul. This connection between spiritual life and modesty exists because the virtue is not just about outward appearances; instead, it is tolerance first and foremost about the inward state of having modesty before God – meaning an awareness of divine presence everywhere and at all times that leads to propriety within oneself and in one's most private moments. Outward modesty means behaving in a way that maintains one's self-respect and the respect of others, whether in dress, speech or behaviour. Inward modesty means shying away from any character or quality offensive to God. The outward is a reminder of the inward, and the inward is essential to the outward.

Modesty permeates most monotheistic faiths

Modesty is not uniquely an Islamic requirement. It's also part of other monotheistic religions. For example, ultra-orthodox Jewish women wear wigs to cover their hair. Nuns wear apostolic as a sign of their religious consecration. Episcopalian women are supposed to wear hats to church. The Qur'anic view of an ideal society is that social and moral values have to be upheld by both Muslim men and women, and there is justice for all, that is, between men and women. The Qur'an asks women to behave with dignity and decorum, befitting a secure, self-respecting and self-aware human being rather than an insecure female who feels that her survival depends on her ability to attract or persuade those men who are interested not in her personality but only in her sexuality.

For women who observe hijab, it is not merely a piece of cloth nor a symbol of defiance. Instead, it is a path that aids self-purification and nearness to their creator. It is a means to teach modesty. A veil is a genuine expression of a woman's religiosity.

Paradoxically, women engaging in the modern world rely on the veil to signal to others that they will express their freedom.

The unrelenting discourse that focuses only on the veil worn by Muslim women gives an oversimplified version of Islam's teachings. A woman can wear a hijab in the West as a sign of modesty yet embrace all of the rights and opportunities Western women enjoy. National policies and media discourses aside, there are endless millions of Muslim women who believe that covering their hair is religiously mandated, so they demonstrate their loyalty to Islam and their relationship with God.

To insist otherwise is to deny the agency, autonomy, and choice of these Muslim women. We can't cast the choices of the hundreds of millions of women who have worn the headscarf as somehow invalid, irrational, wrong, or backwards. Just as women should be free and empowered to choose not to wear the hijab, they must also be free and empowered to wear it if that's what they want. Through this knowledge, women can assert their rights and challenge patriarchal interpretations of slam. While giving priority to a literal, puritanical reading of the Qur'an, they want to discard the historical reality of the Muslim world in favour of the ideal society of Prophet Muhammad and his companions. Their unifying vision has made collective action possible.

Muslim society needs gender parity

Women scholars taught judges and imams, issued fatwas, and travelled to distant cities. Some made lecture tours across the Middle East. The Qur'an's messages of equality resonated in the teaching that women and men have emerged from a single self and are each other's guides who have the mutual obligation to enjoin what is right and to forbid what is wrong. None of the inspired women who were strong, vocal, and fighting for their rights during the era of the Prophet felt that their faith was at odds with their conviction that they, as women, should be equal citizens.

Women do not accept that being feminist means being Western and believe that Western women should be respectful of other paths to social change. Western thinkers and practitioners must reconsider their assumptions about the role of Islam in women's rights and approach this topic with a more nuanced lens.

They must understand the necessity of recognising and consciously accepting the broad cultural differences between Western and non-Western conceptions of autonomy and respecting social standards that reflect non-Western values. Muslim women must work in full partnership with Muslim men, rejecting Western models of liberation but also, and more importantly, asserting their ownThere is no denying the fact that the Muslim world has a significant amount of ground to cover to protect women's rights and freedoms, and the quest for gender equality remains paramount. However, the idea that all Muslim women's liberation is a result of misogynist Muslim men is wide off the mark.

After all, women's oppression manifests itself in several ways. Not all Muslim men are the oppressors.

The protagonists of the Western brand of feminism should heed what the then First Lady Michelle Obama expressed to hijab-wearing students when she told them: "You wonder whether anyone ever sees beyond your headscarf to see who you are, instead of being blinded by the fears and misperceptions in their minds. And I know how painful and frustrating that can be."

* * * * *

9. POLYGAMY IS ISLAM'S SAFETY NET, NOT A PRACTICE

There have been several Muslim customs and practices which have undermined the status of Muslim women—one of them is the custom of polygamy. Polygamy is mainly on the decline and is more of an exception than an accepted or widespread practice. This religious provision is misunderstood primarily in its fundamental role in Muslim society. Polygamy is defined broadly to capture those who have a "conjugal union" with more than one person at the same time. Another definition is "cohabitation with two or more women on the basis of a common household." We must understand that the Islamic provision of polygamy has a humanitarian objective. The provision is an exceptional safety valve for rare and compassionate circumstances. Unfortunately, it is a unique and revolutionary social safety and security net tarnished because of its abuse. The issue of polygamy requires a much-nuanced understanding, and it would be wise that the State leaves it untouched lest it gives credence to the worst fears of one-fifth of its population – the possibility of extinguishment of their cultural identity. Polygamy needs a nuanced understanding to gauge its more profound philosophy and social objective.

The simple truth is that marriage isn't always about love, and love isn't always about marriage. There are lots of cases where people enter into arranged marriages without there ever being any sense of love when they marry. Some people love each other profoundly and never intend to marry. But the real problem is when we say that all love is equal.

Polygamy can also be analysed using the example of the patriarch Abraham among the three great monotheistic religions: Judaism, Islam, and Christianity. Overall, Jews and Muslims have allowed limited polygamy and regulated its practice, while Christians have primarily rejected it. Jews and Muslims have mandated that wives need equality and fairness. Yet there was also controversy in all of these faiths about its practice, with some Christians considering situations in which it might be appropriate and some Jews and Muslims, including wives and their families, seeking to limit polygamy.

Polygamy is a piece of Islamic social legislation

Polygamy is permissible in Islam under strict rules and regulations, but it is misused. Several women argue that their lives became upside-down when their husbands entered multiple marriages. The new code promises a significant reform rooted in India's 1950 constitution, which aims to modernise the country's Muslim personal laws and guarantee complete equality for women. The Qur'anic institution of polygamy is a piece of social legislation which was designed not to gratify the male sexual appetite and lust but to correct the injustices done to widows, orphans, and other female dependants, who are especially vulnerable. It ensured that unprotected women were decently married, old, loose, irresponsible liaisons of men were closed, and morality was restored and upheld. Islam was once receptive to almost every misogynist custom it encountered in the grand march out of Arabia. Polygamy, the veil, and the seclusion of women come not from the Qur'an but from local customs that the prophet's early followers eagerly embraced as part of the Islamic tradition.

The primary concern of the Qur'an was orphans. The Qur'an is the only book with many verses overflowing with profuse compassion for orphans. There can be no better manifesto for the rights of orphans. Polygamy, in the Qur'anic context, implies that there has to be a relationship between the woman or woman whom the Muslim man marries and the orphans because marrying a woman unrelated to orphans will not help safeguard their rights.

While doing justice to orphans is mandatory, so also is doing justice to all the women whom a Muslim man marries. A Muslim family unit is built on the Islamic notion that the husband must always be the primary breadwinner and the wife must always be the primary caregiver. Polygamy, then, is permitted by the Qur'an – not readily but reluctantly as a last resort – and only in conditions of great social hardship and for humanitarian purposes. It is imperative to note that there are two commandments to do justice and that polygamy was allowed for the benefit of orphans and the women who were their guardians or caretakers.

There are two countries which have banned polygamy, while several countries have imposed restrictions on them. Turkey was the first Muslim country to ban polygamy in 1926 legally. This decision has several logical reasons. Instead, it was an entirely secular ban. Tunisia was the following country that banned polygamy through legislation passed in 1956 and restated in 1964. In other Muslim countries, it is restricted by tagging stringent conditions for those going for it. In Pakistan, no man, "during the subsistence of an existing marriage, can contract another marriage without the permission in writing of the Arbitration Council". At the same time, many second wives complain about how neglectful their husbands are toward them and their children, especially in terms of financial support.

Polygamy helps in addressing the problem of deception. Why, in the liberal 21st century, must we live a lie in relationships? And why do we continue to maintain a facade that monogamy is a perfect institution when studies consistently reveal that most men admit to having affairs? Monogamy is great, but it is not for everybody. Islam strongly acknowledges this fact of human nature and stipulates a regulatory framework for plural unions. However, modern Western society does not recognise the qualities of Muslim marriage and family.

Legally enforceable monogamy was an innovation of Emperor Justinian in the year 534. Justinian himself kept a courtesan as a mistress. He married her after the death of his wife, Euphemia, and only after he convinced Justin, his predecessor, to change the law that polygamy became a legal medium for marrying actresses and courtesans.

Justinian is said to have criminalised plural unions under the influence of St Augustine. However, Augustine clearly stated in his treatise on marriage that having several wives is not "contrary to the nature of marriage". Yet, like other religious preachers, Augustine preferred celibacy, or monogamous marriage, if one could not be celibate.

What does the Indian uniform code mean?

The Indian version of the code, primarily driven by the saffron parties and believers in Hindutva ideology, means that there will be a single set of laws for all state residents, irrespective of religion, sex, gender and sexual orientation, on matters such as marriage, divorce, inheritance and adoption. India has embarked on this reform, and several provincial governments have legislated the code.

It will override the different laws and customs practised by Hindus, Muslims, Christians and other minority groups currently on various personal matters. The new law bans polygamy and sets a uniform age for marriage for men and women – 21 and 18, respectively – across all religions and also includes a uniform process for divorce.

India, the world's most populous nation with more than 1.4 billion people, is home to around 80 per cent Hindus and 14 per cent Muslims. Muslims All India Muslim Personal Law Board, the key spokesperson and representative of Muslim religious laws and traditions, believes that the law goes against India's principle of diversity and is "inappropriate" and "unnecessary". According to most Muslims, the bill goes against the principle of diversity. Its primary target appears to be Muslims, especially since even (some Indigenous tribes) remain out of the code. Muslims feel it is a horrible idea, and it is wrong to paint this as gender parity. In short, they are blaming injustice against women on different religious laws when the reason is patriarchy!

Although criminal laws are the same for all, different communities – the majority Hindus (966 million), the country's Muslim (213 million) and Christian (26 million) minorities, and tribal communities (104 million) – follow their civil laws, influenced by religious texts and cultural mores. Religious minorities and tribal communities fear that a uniform code would rob them of their constitutional rights to freedom of religion and culture by imposing a state-determined set of dos and don'ts.

Irrespective of the fine print of a UCC, a uniform code would fundamentally break with India's approach to secularism, which, unlike the West, has primarily allowed different communities to follow their religious practices on matters mandated by their scriptures. Political scientists argue that while personal laws need an upgrade, the path towards any UCC must run through consensus. Without that, the law is little more than a political move geared towards the election – with potentially dangerous consequences for the world's largest democracy.

It does not mean religious laws do not need to be changed. Of course, they should keep up with the times. However, it must be within the framework of those religious laws. The state must remain responsive to the diversity of customs among various communities and not take recourse to it as a ground for queering the communal pitch. It must ensure that one set of rules is not uniform and standardised for all religions.

For all the pontification on women's rights, if this does come to pass, what will come about is the state's version of "modern values". Muslims have been caught in both jeopardy and impasse as a calibrated approach may not yield outcomes favourable to Muslims. There is a need for the warring actors to negotiate and navigate a way out of the stalemate so that they alter the trajectory of the present course of confrontation. The state must assert its independence and non-partisanship. In a vibrant and argumentative democracy like ours, most individuals have a political ideology or inclination. Aristotle said human beings are political animals. As politicians and instruments of governance, they receive both praise and criticism, commendations and critiques. However, they must continue to remain moral bulwarks to protect the Constitution. They must safeguard the truth and dignity of this philosophy.

A solution or privilege

The objective is to solve some social problems with more complex or unwelcome results unless such a possibility is necessary. Take the example of a wife who is suffering from a chronic illness that limits her ability to fulfil her tasks in the usual way. Her husband does not like to divorce her as she is dear to him, and he cares for her welfare. Moreover, divorce would put her in a more difficult position. He wants to retain their marital relationship, but there may be compelling reasons that require the presence of another woman so that the family can function better. It is particularly true when the family includes young children whose mother cannot meet their needs.

In numerous other situations, a second marriage seems to be the better solution for family problems. However, men sometimes have a different view of this situation, which Islam allows. People speak of a man's right to marry more than one wife even though all the texts that speak of it in the Qur'an and the Sunnah stress do it with great caution.

The Prophet lived at a time when continual warfare produced a large number of widows who had no provision for themselves and their children. In these circumstances, polygamy was encouraged as an act of charity. The widows were not necessarily sexy young women but usually mothers of up to six children, who came as part of the deal.

On this point, Muslim law is more elastic and more in harmony with the requirements of society than the other systems of law, which do not permit polygamy in any case. Supposing there is a case in which a woman has young children and falls chronically ill, becoming incapable of doing the household work. The husband cannot employ a maid-servant for the purpose, not to speak of the natural requirements of marital life. She also supposed that the sick woman consented to her husband to take a second wife and that a woman was agreeable to marry the individual in question.

Western would permit immorality rather than a legal marriage to bring happiness to this afflicted home. Muslim law is nearer to reason, for it admits polygamy when a woman herself consents to such a kind of life. The law does not impose polygamy but only permits it in some instances. Polygamy is not the rule but an exception.

The worst tragedy for a woman is when her husband passes away, and, as a widow, the responsibility of maintaining the children falls upon her. In the Eastern world, where a woman does not always go out to earn her living, the problems of widowhood are indescribable. Prophet Muhammad upheld the cause of widows. Most of his wives were widows. In an age when widows were rarely permitted to remarry, the Prophet encouraged his followers to marry them. He was always ready to help widows and urged his followers to do the same.

The social concept of polygamy

The key verse of the Qur'an that legitimized polygamy came after the battle of Uhud, in which the Muslims not only lost against the pagans but also several men died, and there were a large number of widows. Similarly, we have lost more than 90,000 people in the Syrian civil war, which has left so many widows and orphans. In this historical context also, the Qur'an asks men first to consider taking care of orphans, and only when they think they may not be able to do justice to the interest of orphans' s while staying alone should they consider marrying their widowed mothers on the condition that the new family would receive a just treatment and is on par with a typical family that fulfils all necessary social and family obligations.

If the rights of Muslim women are advanced as contained in the spirit of the Qur'an, then the justice that it embodies will never be ignored. Islam does not allow a husband to act cruelly to his wife, either physically or mentally. "O you who believe! You are forbidden to inherit women against their will. Nor should you treat them harshly. On the contrary, live with them on a footing of kindness and equity. If you take a dislike to them, it may be that you dislike a thing which God brings about through it a great deal of good" (Q 4:19)

The plurality of wives made sense during the war when there were many widowed women, and sometimes, they fell on hard times. It was also a sociological mechanism to ensure that men with barren wives could marry again and reproduce. It was certainly not a licence for lust, as suggested by the orientalist fantasy of the harem.

Polygamy may lead to jealousy among wives. We are all human. But in a caring and sharing world where we become euphoric when we give to those in need, sponsor orphans and provide foster care, the ultimate in giving is for a woman to give a fraction of her husband's time and affection to another woman who is willing to share with her. It is a spiritually rewarding experience that allows women to grow while the husband sincerely tries to provide for more than one partner.

In most cases, the husband ends up providing independent accommodation. The women can agree to share dwellings – it's entirely up to them. Many men in Western society complain about their mother-in-law or a "nagging" wife. If his wife and in-laws were hard, would he seek more of the same? The willingness of a man to take on another wife is a form of praise to his first wife if understood correctly in its Qur'anic context. Polygamy was a grave responsibility for Muslim men. In practice, however, it has often been regarded as a male privilege intended for the pleasure of men—the stringent conditions that traditional interpreters have generally disregarded the Qur'an tags to polygamy.

Equal treatment for all wives

It is well-known that Islam allows polygamy within certain conditions, Islam stipulates rigorous equality in the treatment of wives. If a man cannot treat his wives equally, the Qur'an says he should have only one. Monogamy is the norm in Muslim communities. However, men capable of supporting multiple partners must strive to be open, honest, and accountable in their relationships and treat their wives fairly.

"If ye fear that ye shall not be able to deal justly with the orphans, marry women of your choice, Two or three or four; but if ye fear that ye shall not be able to deal justly (with them), then only one, or (a captive) that your right hand possesses, that will be more suitable, to prevent you from doing injustice (or in order not to make your family support worse)" (Q4: 3).

The verse goes on to add that: "You are never able to be fair and just as between women, even if it is your ardent desire..." (Q 4:129)

A man may be married to no more than four wives simultaneously. However, he must maintain fairness between his wives at all times. He may not show favouritism to any one of them. He must give them all the same type of accommodation and standard of living, dividing his time equally between them and meeting all their needs equally and fairly, and he cannot displease any of them. It is a challenging task that most people may be unable to fulfil. Yet, it is obligatory. The attainment of equality in feelings of love and fairness is beyond any person's control. Therefore, God clarifies that people married to more than one wife should not go strongly in favour of one of their wives. They should try hard to moderate their feelings so that no wife feels discriminated against or neglected.

During the prophet's time, men were marrying women in their hundreds. For Islam to restrict the number of wives to a maximum of four was very conservative for the time but also reflective of the lack of property and inheritance rights available to women, rights which Islam went on to afford. Relationships need to be neutral and fair. The concept of fairness demands that a husband treat all his wives with complete and unfailing kindness, showering on each his equal and undivided attention. The husband needs to provide for the physical, emotional, and monetary, in effect, the complete "worldly" welfare of his wives without making any allowance for a compromise or favouring of one spouse. At least two generations ago, polygamy was, indeed, reasonably commonplace, often in the instance where a wife is unable to bear any children. Now, indeed, in South Asia and across the Muslim world, it is anathema.

Anything short of this would be considered a transgression of the Qur'an's recommendation for observing justice. It is not possible, which leads us to believe that polygamy was never meant to be practised and is only done so by men exploiting Qur'anic teachings. The Prophet Muhammad said: "Whosoever has two wives, and he inclines towards one to the exclusion of the other, he will come on the Day of Judgment with his body dropping or bending down. It is truly a mission impossible. There is no place for polygamy in modern society. There are several cases we have come across, and there is hardly a case where a man can balance all the duties required in a polygamous situation.

Modern models of polygamy

In today's industrial society, observing the conditions laid down by the scriptures is impossible. But, social psychologists will say polygamy is a solution to many complex and challenging situations, and, in the absence of a socially sanctioned mechanism, extra social arrangements have to be aligned systematically with cultural and religious norms.

Traditional models of polygamy in a minority of societies) tend to reflect social inequalities between genders, generations and classes. Polygamy not only means that women in polygamous relationships receive a small fraction of a man but that some unfortunate men lower down the pecking order will get no woman at all. But there are perhaps more equitable modern models of polygamy and polyandry emerging in which men and women who are social equals enter into complex relationships that go beyond the nuclear family through which they hope better to fulfil their emotional and physical needs.

Polygamy protects the status of women by giving them full rights. Instead of being a secret "mistress", she becomes a dignified wife with all the rights and privileges that come with being a wife. The compelling message of the Qur'an is that polygamy is a provision for the welfare of widows and orphans and certainly not for the convenience of men. If the overriding concern is the welfare of people in need, polygamy has an enduring relevance. The state's agenda in imposing a uniform code is not limited to activism. It is an outright overreach. A deeper analysis, shorn of a political objective, will bring out the fundamental nature of the social safety valve that polygamy has in mind for the adherents of Islam.

Scriptures have evolved for human societies. But there will always be animal spirits in them. We have the tools for taming them, laws for punishing them, and norms for shaming them. Let us not throw the baby out with the bathwater in our imperfect understanding or prejudice.

* * * * *